T0388424

Diasporic Mobilities on Vacation

Diasporic Mobilities on Vacation is a nuanced exploration of the embodied and affective practices of Moroccans from Europe visiting Morocco for summer vacation. Rather than characterizing them as uncomfortably split between homelands, this book focuses on how their touristic leisure practices create their own space of diasporic belonging.

An expert on Moroccan diaspora communities and mobile lifestyles, the book draws on multi-sited and mobile ethnographic research to take the reader along on the journey 'home' and experience the daily lives of diasporic visitors. Their practices, activities, and encounters on vacation offer insights into larger issues of class, leisure consumption, and transnational belonging in South-to-North migration contexts. Concretely, the book shows how these holiday encounters simultaneously generate integration into Morocco for migrant descendants who can feel at 'home' in this homeland, and differentiation from others in how they embody 'Moroccaness' as social and material actors.

This book shows how seemingly frivolous practices of leisure have material consequences for individuals who belong across homelands. Positioned at the intersection of migration studies, leisure and tourism mobilities, and ethnomethodology and practice theory, this book is a worthwhile read for scholars and students – indeed, anyone questioning or experiencing problems of belonging in transnational and diasporic contexts.

Lauren B. Wagner is Associate Professor in Diasporic Mobilities at Maastricht University, where she serves as Programme Director for the MA Globalisation and Development and as a curriculum developer in the Bachelor in Global Studies. She is a postdisciplinary social scientist investigating diasporic mobilities through ethnomethodology.

Diasporic Mobilities on Vacation

Tourism of European-Moroccans at Home

Lauren B. Wagner

Routledge
Taylor & Francis Group

LONDON AND NEW YORK

First published 2023
by Routledge
4 Park Square, Milton Park, Abingdon, Oxon OX14 4RN

and by Routledge
605 Third Avenue, New York, NY 10158

Routledge is an imprint of the Taylor & Francis Group, an informa business

© 2023 Lauren B. Wagner

British Library Cataloguing-in-Publication Data
A catalogue record for this book is available from the British Library

ISBN: 978-1-032-00028-2 (hbk)
ISBN: 978-1-032-00029-9 (pbk)
ISBN: 978-1-003-17238-3 (ebk)

DOI: 10.4324/9781003172383

Typeset in Times New Roman
by SPi Technologies India Pvt Ltd (Straive)

This book is dedicated to Nora Achrati, my soulmate and eternal editor, without whom I never would have gotten on that first ferry to Morocco.

Contents

Illustrations

Figures

Tables

Map

Fieldnote extracts

Conversations

Foreword

Moving beyond Eurocentric tourist studies

by Tim Edensor

Despite the recent surge in tourism from non-Western countries, non-Western travelers are overwhelmingly construed as moving to Europe and North America, not as tourists but as migrants, exiles, domestic servants, students, and refugees. They express little desire for exploration, adventure, and self-development, unlike the ever-curious, adventurous tourists from the west. These normative scholarly assumptions about tourism are undergirded by Eurocentric, over-general and functional theories in which contemporary tourists are impelled by particular motivations. Tourists, it is suggested, seek to wallow in liminal spaces, discover an authenticity absent from their own societies, or gaze romantically upon exotic other people. Similarly, recent studies identify backpacker motivations to seek novelty, escape routine, acquire cultural capital, develop the self, and, inevitably, quest for 'authenticity'. Such circumscribed explanations have frequently been accompanied by various typologies that identify tourists as belonging to one category or another, immutably consigning them to a classificatory status.

As John Towner argues (1995: 340), "[s]o far, all we have studied is a Western model of tourism evolution, not how it has varied in different cultures and different times." Lamentably, these Eurocentric theories have failed to acknowledge the specific cultural contexts from which tourist motivations and practices emerge; they are therefore unable to recognize the plurality of tourisms in diverse localities and at various times. The result has been, as Victor Alneng (2002: 137) remarks, a "relative indifference towards, and sometimes complete denial of, non-Western tourism." Nonetheless, studies of contemporary non-Western tourism are starting to proliferate. Notable works include much work on Chinese and South-East Asian tourists (Tucker and Hayes 2021; Chang 2021), research into African tourism (Mkono 2011), and mid-twentieth-century Indian tourist explorations (Edensor and Kothari 2018).

With the rise of these diverse accounts, it seems timely to more assertively apply Dipesh Chakrabarty's (2000) proclamation that we need to "provincialize Europe" by problematizing, deconstructing, and decentring the mooted universality of Western knowledge – in this case, of Western tourist theories – while simultaneously multiplying accounts of how tourism is done otherwise in other contexts by other people. Lauren Wagner's compelling, nuanced, and empirically rich study of Moroccan diasporic vacationers provides an exemplary case study of the shifting process through which tourism is performed over several years by a distinctive group of tourists. *Diasporic Mobilities on Vacation: Tourism of European-Moroccans at Home* is all the more powerful for having been produced by driving with tourists to their destinations, accompanying them on their diverse practice while in Morocco, and joining in with their return to Europe. Accordingly, this story is not based on interviews gathered after their travels but during lengthy spells immersed in the field. During her research, the author has evidently developed a sensitivity toward respondents and a rapport with them that has resulted in the accrual of the rich empirical material on display in this book.

This group of tourists, Moroccan diasporic vacationers, further refute reified notions that there is such a thing as *a tourist*, for as Wagner demonstrates, their motivations, practices, and ideals shift over time and across space, and between them: this is a tourism that is continuously becoming. Their holidays are interwoven with changing and diverse practices, informed by intensities of compulsion and desire. They make decisions about whether to stay with relatives according to a shifting sense of obligation, visit renowned national attractions, go shopping, make pilgrimages to ancestral villages, hang around in souks, hit the beach, spend time at the pool, or undertake long evening drives. They vary in the regularity of their vacations, their means of getting there, and their choice of companions. And the experience of the holiday is further conditioned by gender and how this shapes familial obligations and the capacity to travel unattached, engage in leisure activities, and avoid unwanted male attention.

These individual decisions are also accompanied by enduring continuities and shared practices. Diasporic vacationers organize caravans of cars and meet at designated stops along the long journey through France and Spain. They congregate at the same high-quality Moroccan pools, beaches, and cafes. Above all, they share an 'insha'Allah' disposition which accepts the emergence of uncertainty, makes contingent arrangements, and embraces serendipity, an outlook that distinguishes them from those tourists that undertake highly planned, scheduled, and enclavic tours. Their emergent tourist practices are especially encapsulated in the increasing importance of cars as vehicles that transport them to the cafes, beaches, and swimming pools that they patronize together. The car retains an insulated comfort from the inconveniences and hassle of the world outside while facilitating practices of flirting among them when they visit their favorite venues. In Morocco, automobiles are a luxury item owned by a small proportion of the resident population, and the large number of cars occupied by the hypermobile diasporic tourists transform the summer roadscape and mark out their elevated economic status in relation to residents.

Equally importantly, this story of diasporic vacationers demolishes reified notions of migrant identity; indeed, Wagner prefers the concept of 'diasporicness' to emphasize the ceaseless reweaving of connections between their country of descent and country of residence. Relationships with Morocco change as families become more sedimented in European places and older Moroccan family houses disappear. The looseness of their travel decisions and arrangements, the influences of traditions and obligations, and the emergent desires for new pleasures reveal that the diasporic vacationers possess multiple and contested identities. They move between Europe and Morocco, because they have always done so, because this is practically feasible, negotiating their official status as citizens of Europe while always able to claim Moroccan citizenship on the basis of their descent. Wagner's account thus challenges the malign constructions of Fortress Europe and the absurd depictions that distinguish between selves and others. Among the diasporic vacationers, such polarities are meaningless.

To emphasize, the diasporic vacationers are not 'typical migrants' – as if there could ever be such a thing. Their example encourages us to consider other Europeans of diverse descent who similarly forge creative subjectivities as they mediate their different cultural legacies, homes, obligations, beliefs, and enthusiasms. Besides tourism, this ongoing cultural fusing is evident in popular music, film, and fashion, among other areas of creative engagement. Such endeavors and relationalities foreground another Europe that utterly counters the defensive, recursive versions espoused by neo-Nazis and right-wing ideologues. They remind us of Wise and Velayutham's (2014) observation that social researchers tend to focus on problems and points of conflict. Consequently, they ignore positive accounts of everyday interaction in sites of intercultural coexistence and Paul Gilroy's (2004) depiction of convivial cultures. These accounts honor the modest, fleeting ways in which citizens creatively negotiate difference in everyday practice, sharing mundane spaces convivially, affectively, and sensually. The diasporic tourists are emerging from elements of this European convivial culture while simultaneously transforming Europe from within, decentring the claims of those who seek to fix identity over time and space.

References

Alneng, V. (2002). The modern does not cater for natives: Travel ethnography and the conventions of form. *Tourist Studies*, 2(2), 119–142.

Chakrabarty, D. (2000). *Provincializing Europe: Postcolonial thought and historical difference*. Princeton, NJ: Princeton University Press.

Chang, T.C. (2021). "Asianizing the field": Questioning critical tourism studies in Asia. *Tourism Geographies*, 23(4), 725–742.

Edensor, T., and Kothari, U. (2018). Consuming colonial imaginaries and forging postcolonial networks: On the road with Indian travellers in the 1950s. *Mobilities*, 13(5), 702–716.

Gilroy, P. (2004). *After empire: Melancholia or convivial culture?* Oxford: Routledge.

Mkono, M. (2011). African as tourist. *Tourism Analysis*, 16(6), 709–713.

Towner, J. (1995). What is tourism's history? *Tourism Management*, 16(5), 339–343.

Tucker, H., and Hayes, S. (2021). Decentring scholarship through learning with/from each "other". *Tourism Geographies*, 23(4), 704–724.

Wise, A., and Velayutham, S. (2014). Conviviality in everyday multiculturalism: Some brief comparisons between Singapore and Sydney. *European Journal of Cultural Studies*, 174, 406–430.

Acknowledgments

My thanks first and foremost go to the three key women whose participation in this research made it possible. I am indebted to them, their families, and all the other participants who allowed me access to their time, opinions, images, and voices in this project. For their enduring aid in translation, I am indebted to Alexandrine Barontini, Christophe Pereira, and Abdelali Gala. Without their help, my transcripts would be woefully incomplete. Likewise, Tara Rogers did invaluable hard work in compiling and checking the manuscript.

This book collects work I performed in both MA and PhD research activities and in subsequent refining. Various people have been thanked in other documents for their contributions to those, but some deserve to be repeated. Specifically, I credit Christine Deprez, Claire Dwyer, and Ben Page for their support, guidance, and patience as supervisors. Joanna Long and Alan Latham have made my work better as both inner and outer critics. I hope they will be satisfied with the results, but expect that the conversation will be ongoing.

Finally, I hope that Mos, Hedy, and Anouk will be proud of this someday. I hope that Doug Wagner would have been proud. And thanks to Gwyn for watching the baby this morning.

Some of the ideas and empirical data explored in this book have been discussed in my publications elsewhere, in a different format. The following is a bibliography of my work which addresses similar issues as the content of this book. I gratefully acknowledge the peer reviewers, editors, and colleagues whose questions and feedback improved my previous work and this book.

Bidet, J., and Wagner, L. 2012. Vacances au Bled et Appartenances Diasporiques des Descendants d'immigrés Algériens et Marocains en France. *Tracés*, *12*(23), 113–30. https://doi.org/10.4000/traces.5554.

Wagner, L.B. 2008. Diasporic visitor, diasporic tourist: Post-migrant generation Moroccans on holiday at 'home' in Morocco. *Civilisations*, Tourisme, mobilités et altérités contemporaines, *57*(1–2), 191–205.

———. 2015. Shopping for diasporic belonging: Being 'local' or being 'mobile' as a VFR visitor in the ancestral homeland. *Population, Space and Place*, *21*(7), 654–68. https://doi.org/10.1002/psp.1919.

———. 2017a. *Becoming diasporically Moroccan: Linguistic and embodied practices for negotiating belonging*. Clevedon: Multilingual Matters.

————. 2017b. Flirting diasporically: Visits 'home' facilitating diasporic encounters and complex communities. *Journal of Ethnic and Migration Studies*, *44*(2), 321–40. https://doi.org/10.1080/1369183X.2017.1341716.

————. 2017c. Travelling beauty: Diasporic development and transient service encounters at the salon. In Rickly, J., Hannam, K., and Mostafanezhad, M. (Eds.). *Tourism and leisure mobilities: Politics, work, and play*. Abingdon: Routledge.

————. 2017d. Viscous automobilities: diasporic practices and vehicular assemblages of visiting 'home'. *Mobilities*, *12*(6), 827–46. https://doi.org/10.1080/17450101.2016.1274560.

————. 2017e. Mattering moralities: Learning corporeal modesty through Muslim diasporic clothing practices. *Social Sciences*, *6*(3), 97. https://doi.org/10.3390/socsci6030097.

————. 2019. Contingently elite: Affective practices of diasporic urban nightlife consumption. *Urban Geography*, *40*(5), 665–83. https://doi.org/10.1080/02723638.2017.1390722.

Wagner, L.B., and Peters, K. 2014. Feeling at home in public: Diasporic Moroccan women negotiating leisure in Morocco and the Netherlands. *Gender, Place & Culture*, *21*(4), 415–30. https://doi.org/10.1080/0966369X.2013.793658.

Guidance for reading transcripts

This book includes more than 20 tables of transcribed conversations. Together with photographs and ethnographic fieldnotes, which record what I saw and experienced during this ethnography, these transcripts are data of what I heard and said. They were made based on recordings and have been transcribed following Conversation Analysis (CA) conventions.

Any form of transcription involves making choices about how to transform recorded activity into a written format. Many formats of audio transcription focus on words as the main unit to carry meaning. CA transcripts try to include as many elements as possible of human communication, including intonation, emphasis, rhythm, silence, and, when possible, gaze and gesture. So, CA transcripts appear more complicated than other forms of transcribing speech, because they describe more elements of communication than just words. They enable analysis that takes into account how meaning might be understood through the way speech is performed as much as what is said.

Reading CA transcripts takes some practice, as it requires learning an extra set of symbols that describe how the speech sounded in performance, beyond what it expressed in words. It may be easier to read CA transcripts aloud in order to perform both the words that were said and the way they were said. The notation conventions in Table 0.1 indicate which symbols are used to express elements beyond words in my transcripts. These elements include intonation, elongation, emphasis, pauses, silences, overlaps, and changes between a main code (e.g., English) and a secondary code (e.g., Dutch) in the course of speaking. Unfortunately, I did not have video recordings, so there is no information transcribed about gaze or gesture.

In addition, this book uses at least four languages: English, French, Dutch, and Moroccan Arabic or Darija. English, French, and Dutch have been transcribed following dictionary conventions for spellings. Moroccan Arabic speech is transcribed and transliterated, using Roman letters following ISO 233 conventions. The sole exception is the letter jīm, ج, which is transcribed as 'j' instead of 'g' in reflection of Moroccan pronunciation. /g/ is a separate phoneme in Moroccan Arabic, reflecting velarization of the Arabic letter qaf, ق,

Table 0.1 Notation for recorded transcripts

xx	inaudible
?	intense rising intonation
،	slight rising intonation
.	intense falling intonation
/	slight falling intonation
:	elongated vowel or geminated consonant
bold	emphasis
° __ °	lower volume
[	overlap
(),(1.2)	brief pause, pause timed in seconds
(( ))	explanatory or descriptive remark; short translation
<__>	uncertain transcription
normal	main (matrix) language of conversation
underline	secondary Moroccan language
italic	secondary European language
____ *	usage error
#	nonverbal noise created by speaker

Table 0.2 Romanization of Arabic

Character	*Arabic letter*	*IPA symbol*
t̲	ث	θ
j	ج	d͡ʒ
ḥ	ح	h
h̬	خ	x
d̲	ذ	ð
š	ش	ʃ
ṣ	ص	sˤ
ḍ	ض	dˤ
ṭ	ط	tˤ
z̧	ظ	ðˤ
ʿ	ع	ʕ
ġ	غ	ɣ
ı̧	ء	ʔ
ə	(short vowel)	ə

or alternately the phonemic influence of Amazigh languages. Other letters not common in English are listed in Table 0.2. The remaining consonants follow English pronunciation. Long vowels and dipthongs have been simplified and standardized for ease of reading.

1 Introduction

Home for summer vacation

C'est déjà les grandes vacances. Cet après-midi, j'ai vu la famille Ali embarquer pour le Maroc. Ils ont une grande camionnette rouge et tous les ans, ils traversent la France et l'Espagne pour rejoindre le bled et y passer deux mois. Je les regardais depuis ma fenêtre. Ils ont mis au moins une heure à tout préparer. Les enfants étaient bien habillés. On lisait sur leur gueule la joie et l'excitation de partir. Je les enviais. En tout cas, ils ont emmené une tonne de bagages. Les trois quarts des sacs devaient être remplies de cadeaux pour la famille, les amis et les voisins. C'est toujours comme ça que ça se passe. La mère Ali a même emporté un aspirateur. Un Rowenta dernier modèle. Elle va en jeter avec ça là-bas.[1]

(Guène 2004, 105)

This is a story of an annual holiday. It is not my story but one that I am reshaping and diffracting through my encounters with others: persons born and/or raised in France, Belgium, and the Netherlands, of two Moroccan parents, who choose to continue visiting Morocco as adults. I am telling this story in order to investigate how this holiday, these face-to-face encounters, and this cyclical mobility practice is important to understanding, in practical terms, what it means to be actively between places – to be 'from' somewhere, but simultaneously not.

This project connects plentiful research discussions on integration, economic status, and systematic ethnic or religious discrimination of migrants and migrant-origin citizens in the Global North with approaches to the fundamental role of tourism and leisure mobility in shaping and enabling social life. Discussions around the former topic tend to portray this and similar migrant populations in stasis in their roles as 'minorities,' struggling to succeed against largely unwelcoming hegemonic publics. Often, they are simultaneously seen as 'unwelcome' or problematic in their presumed 'homeland' – often never having lived there, but only knowing that place through the practices they learned from their parents, their contact with extended family, and sometimes through visiting. Using a mobilities perspective to take a closer look at this story of a summer holiday magnifies the factor of visiting as an act of leisure consumption: how does the act of travel

DOI: 10.4324/9781003172383-1

and the time spent visiting shape 'belonging' for these diasporic populations? How do they learn how to 'belong' when they visit regularly or irregularly, and how does the place they visit – their ancestral homeland and its residents – respond to them? What do they actually <u>do</u> while on holiday there?

In these discussions, categorization matters: framing their practices and actions through one set of discourses or another changes how we might perceive their trajectory. Instead of treating these individuals as 'migrants,' I prefer to treat them as diasporically mobile: not only as consumers of global medias or 'ethnic' products that connect them to a homeland, but as individuals who participate in visceral, physical, circular movement from homelands in the Global North to a place of origin in the Global South. And on the flip side, instead of treating them as 'tourists,' which might equally be a word to describe people who arrive to spend their summer holidays in leisure activities and then leave, I call them 'visitors' to acknowledge that their connection to that place goes deeper than only leisure. I contend that they are not only going 'back' to visit a place they feel at home but also moving forward in how their visits are a moment of contact between them and the place that they visit – changing both the place and their own lifecourses through these shared experiences.

The seasonal mobile practice of visiting Morocco is a site where the approximately one million post-migrant generation[2] European-Moroccans who choose to travel each summer, hereafter referred to as diasporic visitors (DVs), can feel ethnically linked to everyone around them, practice their Moroccan languages, interact with extended family, experience the sense of public space in a Muslim country, and occasionally meet their spouses and get married. In short, it is as much a site of milestone experiences in their lives as their European homes, and as much a site of contested belonging. In order to illustrate how this holiday fits into an imagination of what it means to be Moroccan in this part of Europe, I reproduce the earlier quote as an item from popular culture where departing on summer holidays is a key moment in European-Moroccan lives.

In this passage from *Kiffe kiffe demain*, Faïza Guène describes the view from the window watching a neighboring family leave on holiday in the voice of an impoverished French Moroccan teenager. Part of her narrator's despondence at their departure comes from the absent presence of her father, who left for the *bled* – from the Arabic word for 'land,' 'countryside' or 'homeland' – abandoning herself and her mother to marry another woman and produce a son. Amid the myriad hypocrisies and frustrations of her state-monitored life, taking place in a predominantly migrant-occupied periurban public housing complex, she and her mother are economically unable to travel. Instead, she witnesses other families piling luggage onto their cars, excited to go.

This example encapsulates this mobile practice as a cyclically recurring story: the palpable presence of the holiday, even for those who cannot join it, and the place it occupies in a European imagination. She describes the iconic overloaded car, packed with goods to take 'home' to support a parallel – possibly better – life taking place there. Both in my discussions with DVs and in much public discourse, such iconic, nostalgic, reverential imaginings of returning to the homeland are important because they are visible to the surrounding community of Moroccans and other Europeans, and because they can present a 'way out' of stigmatization – a voyage toward feeling 'at home.' Without a doubt, the ritual of the holiday creates a specific presence of Morocco in Europe, both for those who take part in it and for those who witness the departures and returns of their families, friends, and neighbors.

Yet, the fact of visiting the 'ethnic' home is not a simple 'return to origins.' As time passes, all of the actors change. The migrants themselves, their families at home, and their children born and raised abroad all adapt to different modes of living that are influenced and reacting to contact with one another; but also the places they come from, the places they live, and their connections to one another shift over time and contact. When migrants started making this journey in the 1970s, air travel was prohibitively expensive; now low-cost options connect cities across Europe with cities across Morocco, and traveling by car is no longer the default option. That change, too, works itself into how these individuals perpetuate a connection to a diasporic 'home.'

With these issues in mind, in this book, I investigate how these summertime DVs 'belong' – and not – in Morocco. In both their homes in Europe and in Morocco, the diasporic act of visiting 'home' is framed by an imagination of Morocco as a 'homeland' where they might in some way 'return' and 'belong,' but when there, they often encounter a sense of 'strangeness,' of not quite fitting what they think, or what others think, they should be as 'Moroccans.' This complex belonging is even evoked in the colloquial term sometimes used to refer to this group in Moroccan Arabic: *magharba min el-kharij*, or just *kharij*, meaning 'Moroccans from outside' or 'outsiders.' Rather than using this formulation, which defines them in relation to territorial Morocco, I use 'diasporic' as a categorization through which we might understand how these individuals are assembling something new from their engagement and enmeshment in multiple places. It is not something that can be defined additively, as a combination of different parts, but *cumulatively*, as elements entwining over time and across space to become 'more-than' what came before. Becoming diasporic, then, means intermittently becoming 'same' and 'strange' and also both of them simultaneously – assembling multiple influences and relations from multiple homes and homelands to become more than the sum of one's parts.

To investigate how this works, I disassemble this diasporic practice of visiting home into forces of *embodiments*, *attachments*, and *insulations*. Interweaving them all together here assembles into my analysis of how diasporicness works for a cohort of Moroccan-origin individuals visiting Morocco from Europe. These forces are all co-occurring simultaneously, and so they are not forcibly parsed into individual chapters in this book. Instead, I interlace vignettes of each force in a broadly chronological story about a composite summer holiday in Morocco, from departure to return, formulated through combinations of empirical data gathered over several summers since 2007.

I arrived at these three forces via an ethnomethodological approach to social order, focusing on what becomes relevant to participants as they are 'doing-being' themselves in many different iterations during holidays in Morocco – as people with intensive family connections to the place of Morocco, but also people who want to enjoy their leisure time while on holiday there. These 'doing-beings' involved various forms of material and expressive *embodiment*, from practices of tanning and boredom, to ways of moving through space as part of a 'driver-car.' The *embodiments* vignettes show examples of how DVs are physically and materially experiencing their presence in Morocco, both as individual bodies and as a collective of bodies traveling individually-but-together in parallel rhythms on an annual basis. The practices referring to modes of diasporic *attachment* are those that act both as a positive centripetal force, pulling individuals into visiting Morocco, and as a centrifugal force, pushing them away when the pressure of familial obligation becomes too intense. Vignettes about *attachment* show how DVs are attracted to visit Morocco by a sense of rootedness and sometimes nostalgia, but also actively resist some expectations about how they will spend their time while there. Finally, their 'doing-being' on vacation involves emergent *insulations*, found in how DVs are leisure-seekers, both enthusiastically participating in a 'homeland Morocco' full of their family and friends, and simultaneously, as a collective mass of bodies, reinforcing spaces of exclusivity among their 'own,' 'strange' (diasporic) crowd. *Insulation* vignettes illustrate moments when DVs inhabit spaces where they can hang out among people like themselves – sometimes by purposefully excluding, or being excluded by, others; sometimes through the neutral choices and preferences of individuals that accumulate into an exclusive collectivity.

Before entering into these vignettes, you may choose to read a part-theoretical, part-methodological background for them in the next chapter ("Assembling Diasporicness: More than the Sum of Its Parts"), which describes why I will never talk about 'ethnic' or 'national' 'identity,' but only about emergent categorization based on *descent* and *place* as key nodes in an assemblage approach to thinking about 'diasporicness.' You can also read the methodological practicalities about how the research was done in the appendix ("Appendix: Methodological Design"). Or, you can come back to read those after you have entered the story. Like the people this book discusses, the book itself aims to allow multiple ways in and create something that is more than the sum of its parts.

Notes

1 Author's translation:

> It's already time for the holiday. This afternoon, I saw the Alis leave for Morocco. They have a huge red van and every year they drive through France and Spain to return to the bled and spend two months there. I watched them from my window. They took at least an hour to get ready. The kids were all dressed up. You could read on their faces the happiness and excitement to

leave. I envied them. In any case, they brought a ton of luggage. Three-quarters of the bags must have been full of presents for the family, friends and neighbors. It always happens like that. The mother even brought a vacuum cleaner. Latest model Rowenta. She'll go nuts with it there.

Original text: *Kiffe kiffe demain*, by F. Guène © Hachette Littératures 2004 © LIBRAIRIE ARTHEME FAYARD 2010.

2 I prefer the term 'post-migrant' over 'second' generation following Fouron and Glick-Schiller's (2002) observation that 'second' generation implies that the individuals in question are still in a process of migrating. Post-migrant generation(s), in contrast, refers to the rupture of migration as an event and the contexts it creates in aftermath. The estimate of one million post-migrant generation diasporic visitors is calculated based on population estimates of Moroccans residing in France, Belgium, and the Netherlands (Fondation Hassan II and IOM 2003), along with tabulations by the Moroccan Office of Tourism (Ministére du Tourism 2012) of summer entries of Moroccan Nationals Resident Abroad (accessed 26 October 2010).

References

Fondation Hassan III and IOM (International Organization for Migration). (2003). *Marocains de l'Extérieur*. Rabat: Fondation Hassan II. https://www.iom.int/sites/g/files/tmzbdl486/files/jahia/webdav/shared/shared/mainsite/activities/countries/docs/Marocains_de_l%27ext%C3%A9rieur.pdf.

Fouron, G., and Glick-Schiller, N.G. (2002). The generation of identity: Redefining the second generation within a transnational social field. In Levitt, P., and Waters, M. (Eds.). *The changing face of home: The transnational lives of the second generation*. New York: Russell Sage Foundation Press.

Guène, F. (2004). *Kiffe kiffe demain*. Paris: Hachette Littératures.

Ministère du Tourisme. (2012). *Arrivées des touristes*. Rouyaume du Maroc: Ministère du Tourisme, de l'Artisanat et de l'Economie Sociale et Solidaire. http://www.tourisme.gov.ma/fr/tourisme-en-chiffres/arriv%C3%A9es-des-touristes.

2 Assembling diasporicness

More than the sum of its parts

i Attuning ethnomethodologically on 'diasporicness'

This whole project begins with a paradox. While I have just asserted that there is something called 'diasporicness,' and I intend to disassemble it to discuss how it works, to do so methodologically and theoretically, I have to first establish when and how such a thing might exist. I approach this paradox by using theories about categorization and how categories emerge in practical, ordinary life (Robles 2020), while also questioning if the thing I am looking at, as it is informed and shaped by previous theory, *does* exist. That process has been advocated by some as a responsible approach to social science more broadly (Sassen 2013a, 2013b), but it is first and foremost a key tenet of my main influence, ethnomethodology.

Ethnomethodology is broadly concerned with how actors emergently organize everyday life so that it makes sense to them (Garfinkel 1984; Katz and Csordas 2003; Liberman 2013; Maynard and Clayman 1991). For that approach to work, everything must be considered as 'data,' from the words spoken to the way they are spoken, to the circumstances, present and absent actors, and infinitesimal references they make to other events. All data makes sense to the actors involved; the task of the analyst is figuring out how it makes sense (Katz 1999). Moreover, the analyst must assume that everything is connected to something, though some connections pop out and some are moderately active, while others lie dormant and possibly expire. The back and forth between how things work 'normally' and how actors recognize them to be surprising indicates, for the ethnomethodologist, something about how social life is emergently organized.

So, the task of an ethnomethodological social scientist is to notice how participants make all these different elements relevant in the way they encounter each other. This might entail paying closer attention to certain aspects of life and leaving others behind, based on how research participants orient around organizing life – what elements become 'relevant' to the unrolling of events because they are so profoundly ordinary (things always work this way) or because they violate some assumption about what should happen next (they cause 'trouble' and need 'repair'). In analysis, we can make some observations about which elements are changing together or against one another

DOI: 10.4324/9781003172383-2

(whether mundanely or remarkably), draw some comparative conclusions about the speeds at which they change, and wonder what it might mean for future pathways of what becomes 'normal.'

Ethnomethodological investigations draw on many qualitative methods to collect data, with ethnography being among the most prominent. Ethnography, through an ethnomethodological lens, involves observing and participating – attuning (Latham and Wagner 2021) – to the minutiae of dynamics in everyday life for a targeted group of people, in order to describe how their lives work under 'normal' circumstances. Every ethnographer does this in a slightly different way, with attention to different elements of 'normality,' and with a positioned and reflexive ability to perceive different types of change and transformation. I performed this ethnography after spending significant time in Morocco, starting from my first visit as a tourist in 1999, over several periods doing research and language training there. As I learned how to speak and act in a way where I could 'fit in' in Morocco, I applied that attention to language use in interactions between diasporic and resident Moroccans, by training myself to speak and understand, to the best of my abilities, the different languages involved (principally Moroccan Arabic, French, and Dutch). During fieldwork periods when I was following along with DVs during their summer vacations, during 2003, 2007, and 2008, I was also acclimating myself to being 'on holiday' in the same way that diasporic participants were 'on holiday.'

An ethnographer might also ask others (interview) about their interpretations of how things work. Following Katz (1999: 8), I maintain an empirical distinction between what people do, and what they say about what they do. As much as my own positioning – as an 'outsider' in many dimensions (non-Moroccan, non-European, non-Muslim) – might influence how I interpret my observations, the moment-to-moment interactional and relational interests of participants are inherent to how they characterize what they experience, even if they are 'insiders.' As a result, I tend to focus on what happens first, then look at how participants relate to what is happening, both in that time and space through their commentary in the moment, and through their reflections at later moments, in different circumstances of retelling.

Back to the paradox. Though I entered into research with an idea of 'diasporicness' as being relevant to this activity of going on holiday to Morocco – in that choosing to go to Morocco and not somewhere else with one's summer vacation time indicates a certain amount of value attributed to spending time in Morocco as a homeland – the activities I followed along with during my fieldwork indicated that 'diasporicness' was not necessarily configured toward the 'homeland' in ways I had seen it depicted in other research. Elements like a sense of ethnicity, nationality, or community were important, but 'diasporic Moroccanness' also happened in complex webs of interconnection: how state borders connect the road through Spain to the road in Morocco; how being a visitor means using mental energy to translate between euros and dirhams as much as it means managing 'mentalities' that are seen as different between residents and visitors; and, above all, how expectations for spending time with family conflict with desires to get some sun and hang out with friends. Though going to Morocco is about being connected to a family whose origins are located in Morocco, it is also about more than a family connection. It incorporates ideas about race, identity, migration, transnationalism, tourism, leisure consumption, social class, economic power, globalization, gender, Islam, and linguistic competence, in multifaceted combinations between them. These aspects are all more and less than any single keyword can adequately describe. So, I approach what I observed during this holiday as a social assemblage of many dimensions that happen together (DeLanda 2006), with some happening with more presence (or more absence) than others in different moments of encounter, but all taking place in relation to a presumption of 'diasporicness' connecting the actors involved.

Thus, while 'diasporicness' here might not mean the same as how it has been defined by previous research and theoretical development, it is still a dimension that makes visiting Morocco a 'normal,' ordinary thing to do for the group of people I followed. That is, the various elements that come together to make this visit happen on a regular basis – like the availability of a house to visit in Morocco and the pressure from family members to come along on the trip there – trace back to a diasporic rupture, when parents or grandparents decided, among the many different paths of life they might have chosen, to migrate from Morocco to Europe. The availability of that path is, of course, nested into historical dependencies that stretch far beyond their individual stories – in particular, stories of colonization and economic exploitation by the Global North of the Global South – which I outline briefly in the vignette "Attachments: Generational Mobilities between Morocco and Europe." From an ethnomethodological perspective, however, what matters is that the following generations continue to exercise this practice as an ordinary part of their summer holidays. Irrespective of the fact that this particular vacation involves crossing national borders, it demonstrates how a category of 'diasporicness' is relevant to this group: it is a 'diasporic' practice because its practitioners organize their lives to make the dispersion from a homeplace and the (cyclical, temporary) return to it an ordinary and normal event.

Turning away from some assumptions about migration

When it was enthusiastically pointed out within memory of our present Academy that race or gender or nation…were so many social constructions, inventions, and representation, a window was opened, an invitation to begin the critical project of analysis and cultural reconstruction was offered. And one still feels its power even though what was nothing more than an invitation, a preamble to investigation has, by and large, been converted instead into a conclusion – eg. "sex is a social construction," "race is a social construction", "the nation is an invention," and so forth, the tradition of invention. The brilliance of the pronouncement was blinding. Nobody was asking what's the next step? What do we do with this old insight? If life is constructed, how come it appears so immutable? How come culture appears so natural? If things coarse and subtle are constructed, then surely they can be reconstrued as well? To adopt Hegel, the beginnings of knowledge were made to pass for actual knowing.

(Taussig 1993: xvi)

Now that we can establish that the thing that is going on here involves some kind of 'diasporicness,' we can review what that has meant to other theorists and how they frame the social problems it presents. While I incorporate a broadly agreed definition of 'diasporic' that has to do with dispersion and return, I will propose a different set of assumptions about how social life operates than many of the theorists who have previously discussed 'Diaspora' as a formal category. The differences are important to how I imagine these dynamics to work: I think of 'diasporicness' and 'being/becoming diasporic' as a relational, emergent event rather than an 'identity' (Wagner 2012). I see it as requiring assumptions based in an assemblage approach to social life (DeLanda 2006) rather than the assumptions of the predominantly social constructionist approach espoused by many of the key players in these debates. As Taussig proposes above, I want to take a step further than thinking about diasporic 'identities' as socially constructed and think about how becoming diasporic is emergent and generative in itself.

Many social scientific applications of 'Diaspora' refer to certain historically specific cases of population dispersal, created by mass exodus in relation to crises of historical proportions. These major historical changes range from religious persecution to the global slave trade (Gilroy 1993; Schnapper 1999; Shuval 2000; Tölölyan 1996). Expanding beyond those, 'diaspora' has been used to describe large-scale population movements that might otherwise simply be called 'migration,' in order to focus on modes of attachment to a distant homeland (Anthias 1998; Christou and Mavroudi 2016; Mavroudi 2007; Werbner 2002). In a vein of limiting the expansiveness of the term, Cohen's defining book *Global Diasporas* isolates 'diaspora' from other terms like 'transnational' or 'migrant' as representing only groups that adhere to certain qualities: initial traumatic dispersion, mythologizing and idealizing a homeland, maintaining an 'ethnic group' consciousness in contrast to the dominant local host society, and espousing a desire to return (1997: 180).

Like most restrictions of terms, this one becomes quickly problematic, even just looking at a case like Morocco. Some members of 'The Moroccan Diaspora' might fit into this definition, while others would not, even though they all might be living in the same 'community' outside of Morocco.

Moreover, someone who might fit the requirements for potentially being a 'diaspora' member may change in his or her orientation toward that over a lifetime. Groups that fit these requirements might shift away from acting like a 'diaspora' as members over generations become more attached and 'at home' in the place of settlement rather than longing for the place of ancestral origin. Even if it is an effort to delineate and make this definition useful, its utility is not universal, and perhaps lacks a productive potential to evolve with new waves of change.

Broadly speaking, as well, these definitions are predicated on assumptions about personhood with a holistic idea of 'identity' as somehow part of an 'ethnic' inheritance. Under that assumption, diasporic identities only become feasible as unwieldy 'hybrid' combinations between ancestral and resident homes. These unwieldy 'double' identities engender further assumptions about borders that rely, to a greater or lesser extent, on their cartographic delineations between 'nations' – which, as Taussig mentions, are inventions – and then seek to problematize those delineations. Assumptions about change, likewise, tend to be conceived as linear processes of adding and subtracting parts over historical time. Resulting 'identities' remain, problematically, imagined as *extensive* entities, as units that can be combined or divided into component parts (Delanda 2002: 26) – for example, as if the 'Moroccan' parts of one's lifestyle can be cleanly divided from the 'Belgian' parts, without causing a transformative rupture.

Making these assumptions, I contend, causes more problems than it solves. The authors that rely on them are often obligated to make involved arguments to transform what they observe about 'diaspora' from something grounded in an imaginary of a 'whole' identity compounded from component ideas of 'ethnicity' and 'nationality' as being cartographically-bounded labels into something functionally 'hybrid' (Kalra et al. 2005). That is, they are often working hard to deproblematize, and de-extensivize, hybridity.

Shifting away from these assumptions, and toward assumptions related to life as *intensive* assemblage, builds from a premise of *indivisibility*: that rather than adding and subtracting parts of 'Moroccanness' or 'Belgianness,' these parts are fused into new formations that cannot be subdivided without changing the nature of the entity they became. Considering diasporicness as intensive makes deproblematizing something like 'hybridity' no longer necessary. Rather, multiplicity becomes the starting point for imagining people as all perpetually multiple – intensive, indivisible masses of materialities and expressivities that are only formed in relation to other entities (DeLanda 2006). Rather than 'whole' subjectivities (that might be then extensively divisible into ethnic or national 'parts'), intensive multiplicity means that 'hybridity' is no longer a possible form of 'identity,' much less a problematic one.

Assembling from multiplicity presumes that people become more than the sum of their parts. The experiences, histories, and understandings of being attached to multiple sites become integrated into one's body and life, rather than component parts of it. Sara Ahmed, for example, uses her skin to think about this: she describes her experiences of changing homes from England to

Australia through how her skin "wrinkled" in reaction to each environment (2000: 90) as a way of recognizing how home is lived and felt through the body. "The experiences of migration – of not being in a place one lived as home – are felt at the level of embodiment, the lived experience of inhabiting a particular space, a space that is neither within nor outside bodily space" (2000: 92). Likewise, accepting that 'home' takes place in many spaces simultaneously – topologically through a flat ontological space rather than cartographically across borders (Jones et al. 2007) – means that it is no longer necessary to justify why one can feel 'at home' in spaces that seem distant from each other. Flatness here means that even though places may appear distant, they can be experienced as near in how they are intertwined in one's body. Ordinal, 'flat' timespace unfolds as a sequence of ordered steps linked with one another, like iterations or generations, rather than linearly as additive, causal, or directional (DeLanda 2002, 2006).

Realigning assumptions in this way releases 'diasporicness' from exclusively describing cross-border dispersion, which tends to emphasize 'transnational' border crossings as the position from which one might seek connection to home. Instead, diasporic pull can reflect nostalgic impulses for any kind of distant 'home,' whether it is Sara Ahmed as a 'migrant' or Doreen Massey (2005: 96) longing for the north of England from her position in London academic circles. Each theorist can recognize 'home' diasporically, as pulling both for past moments, affects, and statuses, and for places that are physically at a distance but feel close – whether or not crossing any 'national' border is required to reach them. I suggest thinking about these dispersions, broadly, as a kind of rupture: not necessarily a violent or instantaneous event, but nevertheless an accelerating and decelerating transition from category to category that can only be recognized retrospectively (Latham and Wagner 2021). That rupture opens a potential to look back to how previous lives were shaped – or in the virtual as used by Delanda (2002), how they might have been – and to look forward to how those multiple categorizations create new possibilities.

Observing how that rupture iterates and shifts, and which dimensions of a human multiplicity become implicated in maintaining orbit within one category or another, reorients toward 'diasporicness' as an emerging, multinodal system. Then, instead of developing an argument about how 'identities' of its member entities relate to different poles, we can focus – as I try to do in the following pages – on analyzing how individuals who can position themselves diasporically actively negotiate dimensions of belonging that shape their lives and their worlds. We start from where they emerge, evolve, and perhaps produce something new, rather than starting from their struggle with the status quo.

Descent and place as dimensions of diaspora

In terms of the participants in this research, for whom the rupture (or "phase transition") can be traced more or less precisely to a moment of mass migration from Morocco to Europe, the reconfiguration I propose for 'being/

becoming diasporic' focuses on *descent* and *place* as dimensions that persistently become relevant in this diasporic assembling. Shifting to this terminology from previous metaphors, like 'roots and routes' (Clifford 1997; Levitt 2009) or 'blood and soil' (Brubaker 2002; Glick Schiller 2005; Malkki 1992; Nash 2002), translates my conceptualization of how diaspora works from a social constructionist language about 'ethnicity' and 'nation' to a language of entities moving along trajectories in a systemic assemblage with each other. In this sense, *descent* and *place* are both expressive and material: they are about the framings, discourses, and ideas in combination with tangible and physical manifestations, and how these entities can fuse together or stretch apart and disintegrate. In this section, I will outline a theoretical perspective on how *descent* and *place* can be imagined as dimensions in assemblage working with and against each other through affects and practices, cumulatively moving toward a new equilibrium state of 'diasporicness' following the rupture of migration.

We can imagine a scenario where a community of *descendants* inhabits the same *place* in perpetuity; this is what *descent* and *place* look like working in concert, mapping onto each other in a one-to-one system. Fusing together, they act to solidify and stabilize (territorialize) ideal-typical categories (attractors) of nation-states – like the stereotypes we think of when we imagine 'Moroccanness' or 'Frenchness' or 'Dutchness' – so that underlying assumptions of community continuity remain stable and linear. In this scenario, the ordinal repetition of generations evolves in small, predictable steps rather than broad uncertain leaps.

Imagine, instead, that a rupture has destablized (deterritorialized) these dimensions, so that they are moving in different directions while still reaching for each other, struggling toward a new, more or less stable equilibrium. To use the thermodynamic metaphors of Manuel DeLanda, systems that are close to equilibrium appear static and stable, even though they are in constant motion – much like ideas of 'nationality' that are untroubled and consistent. Systems that are far-from-equilibrium – for instance, a system that has recently experienced a phase transition – demonstrate more variation, providing the means to observe their complexity through their recurring, more dramatic movements. They exhibit dynamics of attraction toward previous states (like an ancestral idea of 'Moroccanness'), other virtual states (the 'what might have been' of alternate possible pathways), and the emergent actualized state – the wobbly motion they engage in while trying to find a new balance together (DeLanda 2002: 66).

Thinking about these territorializations and deterritorializations explicitly in terms of *descent* and *place* enables us to recognize the potency of virtuality – the 'what might have been' – on emergent actuality. Had the linear relationship between *descent* and *place* been maintained in another version of reality, families might have collected together in communities that would not migrate (though they might have changed in other ways). Recognizing how virtual states have influence on actuality means recognizing that imagined life paths that didn't happen have effects on what *did* happen after the rupture of migration. They influence the opinions and attitudes people develop about how that change took place and complicate the evolving relationships of how things develop *nonlinearly* – in ordinal, generational steps, which exponentially accumulate into seemingly unpredictable surges, clusters, and long trails toward new transitions – rather than a linear, additive, more predictable flow of stable continuity.

Using this way of speaking and thinking about dimensions of belonging, rather than 'ethnicity' or 'nationality' as totalizing belongings, helps show how *descent* and *place* can work to locate one's sense of rootedness. It can locate someone like Doreen Massey (cited earlier), who experiences a nostalgic attachment to home while not being considered a 'migrant' as much as the classic modes of 'Diaspora' that presume the crossing of ethnic, national, or religious borders. Treating *descent* and *place* as entities in assemblage shifts attention from how they 'should' be – which is often reported in research on diaspora in terms of how people feel 'detached' or 'in-between' places – toward exploring what new mode of belonging is produced through their new mappings onto, or away from, each other. It is trying to understand what sort of categories emerge through the rupture and repositioning of *descent* and *place* as they seek a new equilibrium. This tension between *descent* and *place* is part of what creates 'diasporic Moroccanness,' in how it emerges unpredictably and suddenly across multiple dimensions of social life that connect with taking a vacation in Morocco.

ii Observing affective practices and leisure as 'diasporic'

One way of observing how these dimensions operate is through experiences of affect. While affect is a term with diverse definitions across psychology, anthropology, human geography, and philosophy, following Margaret Wetherell I think of it as "*embodied meaning-making*" (italics original) based in human emotion that manifests in social life (2012: 4). In this sense, affect is embodied but not individual: it involves ideas, feelings, emotions, and sensations that accumulate within and in relation to other bodies – whether people, things, discourses, or other kinds of interactable beings. Affective modes of being can feel like internal engines within an individual, while being intrinsically entangled with cultural and societal positionings and values, following patterns that connect us with categories of belonging. They can be expressed as much through action and activity – which Wetherell includes within 'affective practice' – as through language, especially since one of the frequently repeated theoretical ideas about affect is that it can be ineffable or inexpressible in language. The feeling of going to a party is one way of understanding what affect does: without really understanding why, or being able to identify what, one can sense the energy, excitement, and enthusiasm of it. Participating in the affective atmosphere generated by a great party might prompt behavior that would be otherwise unusual, as all kinds of human and non-human actors get swept up into it. The 'meaning' of such a party can be described in words, but our understanding of it is enriched by approaching it as an embodied experience and trying to explore what makes it vibrate with feeling when interacting with it.

Affect as part of embodied practices are important to understanding why the summer vacation in Morocco perpetuates for the participants I followed. The things that pull them there are not embodied singularly, within one individual; they are shared among a community. Moreover, they are not always describable emotions; they can be vibrating attractions to and repulsions from different groups, places, sites, and activities as participants travel and circulate in this atmosphere. Examining these as affective practices helps to observe how belonging with 'Moroccanness' as experienced in Morocco perpetuates a path that leads to visiting 'home.'

An example of what I see as an affective practice of diasporicness is what I call 'insha'allah.' As a phrase, it means 'with God's will.' In the way I observed it being talked about and acted upon by participants in this research, it involves serendipity as associated with leisure in a way that contrasts Morocco against a place of European residence. *Insha'allah* becomes an affective practice as a feeling or a state of being that many participants adhered to and sought to produce through their choices for how they visit Morocco. It came to characterize a DV way of visiting Morocco, in contrast to their parents' ways of visiting, because it generated experiences that may be unpredictable and sometimes full of stress, but often surprisingly fun and rewarding afterward. Over time, these experiences accumulated into a discourse about the holiday, repeated to me by many participants, that things always happen last-minute, 'insha'allah' – with the serendipitous will of God. So, I treat *insha'allah* as an affective practice that emerged for Moroccans from Europe (in contrast to other migrant groups) in that they were free from civil wars and other blockages to visiting 'home,' close enough to drive their cars to get there, able to choose to make that trip spontaneously, and swept up through their positive embodied experiences to do it again year after year. Moreover, through viscosity, they were able to participate in *insha'allah* timespaces of socially like-minded DVs spread throughout Morocco. Over time and with repetition, this practice becomes *affective*: filled with and inseparable from the excitement of having fun in a familiar homeplace that is, necessarily, far from home.

Insha'allah is one element of an assemblage that characterizes, I contend, a 'diasporic Moroccanness' in that it evolves a new relationship between *descent* and *place* by perpetuating a far-from-equilibrium mobility. It constitutes a 'new' tradition of diasporic Moroccanness, that might get passed down to further generations and perpetuate a stabilizing community (equilibrium) of Moroccans from Europe. But it is a new practice in an ordinal step from the previous one: it continues how parents and grandparents visited home, and in some ways maintains the connections they made, while also making new connections through new complex and multipolar dynamics of *descent* and *place*. Together, these are forms of leisure consumption that keep DVs together as a unique group as much as they are forms of maintaining a connection to Morocco.

To describe how *insha'allah* and other affective practices pull and push entities that are engaged in them – from individuals, to forms of embodiment, to practices of leisure consumption – I use a metaphor of *viscosity* (Saldanha 2007). *Viscosity* extends the thermodynamic way of thinking I began earlier as a term that describes both how social and material entities stick together and focus around each other, and how they break apart and diffuse through the surface tension created in movement. It helps us think about how entities can repel or absorb others nearby. It enables me to talk about how the fleshy body of a person or the metal body of a car can become both a barrier that separates entities from certain other entities and a magnet that seeks (and finds) others like it. This cumulative form of movement in assemblage, involving bodies, behaviors, and categories in constant motion, describes surges of collectivity and long tails of dispersion that then congeal into something else, rather than linearly definable borders or boundaries between groups.

Saldanha introduces viscosity to describe the way he sees Goa 'freaks' – long-term, semi-resident visitors who occupy and produce the 'scene' of club culture in Goa – separate and reconvene in certain places at certain times, through certain forms of mobility:

> Observing again and again that certain spaces and times tended to attract hippies and ravers, which then made these spaces and times relatively impenetrable for Indians, I needed a concept to account for both the attractive forces between white tourists and the surface tension that enveloped them, without losing sight of the possibility that the boundaries could be (and were regularly) transgressed.
>
> (Saldanha 2007: 49)

Like a viscous liquid, individuals become molecules seeking to join with like molecules and maintaining a membranous surface tension that can keep unlike molecules separate. For DVs specific factors act as attractive forces, much like Saldanha's hippies and ravers, to bind them together: shared language and histories, networks of known people in common, and a similar purpose in coming to Morocco – holiday leisure consumption. Viscosity is thus collectively pushing and pulling, shaping around attractors and against unlike bodies, to aggregate a larger mass of many bodies sticking together. Certain likenesses bind DVs together, while other forces repel them from interacting with locally resident Moroccans. And much of this activity happens while they are mobile – moving from Europe to Morocco and around Morocco as leisure seekers during their summer vacation.

Incorporating mobilities into 'diasporicness'

The final part to assembling 'diasporicness' of this group of Moroccan-origin individuals must take into account the way that they are mobile between Europe and Morocco. This means taking a step outside of research about migration, transnationalism and diaspora and how those literatures define this group in terms of their ancestry and place of residence, to think about how their *mobility* practices are also part of diasporicness. In other words, how they travel, how they seek leisure, how they move around the city, and how they are able to do so – to be mobile across borders – when others may not be.

The mobilities paradigm (Cresswell and Merriman 2011) is a key frame in this project, as the central premise of considering humans as fundamentally mobile rather than static emerges here in multiple realms. First, I consider migration itself as mobility rather than displacement, in thinking about it as one step in a sequence of moves and flows between places (Chapter 3, Section ii – "Attachments: Generational Mobilities between Morocco and Europe") rather than a definitive relocation from one space to another. A mobilities perspective enables me to put migration on a spectrum with tourism, rather than classifying these as completely separate practices, acknowledging how they interlace with each other in enabling circulation between places. Mobilities research plays a further role in exploring the embodied and affective experiences of movement, as they relate to the senses of speed, freedom, and protection of driving a car as well as the frustrations of getting stuck. In fact, the methodological premise of this project to 'follow the people' starts from a mobile perspective – that in order to understand their lives, we as researchers need to practice their mobilities with them (see the appendix for more about mobile methodologies in this research).

In this sense, DV mobility practices between Europe and Morocco – which could otherwise be called 'return migration' – can be alternatively viewed through Morocco's orientation toward attracting tourists. Tourism flows in Morocco tend to adhere to models of 'third world' or 'ethnic' tourism, in that visitors most often come from higher income countries and their expectations include a certain amount of exoticism and Otherness mixed with leisure consumption at a lower price than can be found at home (Minca and Oakes 2006). This perspective, at least in the case of Morocco, is not random: the first French protectorate governor, Lyautey, began development of Marrakech (and other cities) as luxury leisure resorts for French visitors early in the twentieth century (Stafford et al. 1996: 33). That profile has been reinforced by literary and artistic images that perpetuate Orientalist ideologies about Morocco (de Graincourt 2010; Green 1991), as well as by the active production and marketing of Morocco as a tourism destination by the state itself (Minca and Wagner 2016).

Diasporic visitors are not immune to these images, nor to the 'touristic' pursuit of collecting experiences of a place as a way to 'know' it. In some ways, their ability to visit depends upon the fact that many others are visiting – they take the same low-cost flights from all over Europe to the big tourist destinations in Morocco. Yet their relationship with the place is not the same detached stance as the archetypal tourist, which gives the acts of collecting and consuming a different timbre. In some ways, their practices fit more concretely with Visiting Friends and Relatives (VFR), which incorporates diasporic visitors with others who sit outside of the classic 'tourist' proto-type, undertaking the voyage in the context of visiting a person or persons as well as the place (Coles and Timothy 2004; Hollinshead 2004). Research shows that VFR travelers are also consumers. Their consumption might take place in particular ways that differ from other tourists but adhere to a touris-tic logic of spending time in leisure spaces and cultural spaces and pursuing non-essential purchases (Duval 2003: 273), while also being a means to per-form a 'return' to family and ancestral locations (Ali and Holden 2006; Conway et al. 2009; Conway and Potter 2009; Duval 2004).

Yet DV practices of leisure consumption also fit with more banal modes of leisure mobilities, like 'going out' to public spaces of consumption. They involve the safety and danger issues that are often perceived as part of urban nighttime activities (Chatterton and Hollands 2002; Gallan 2015; Shaw 2014), as well as familiarity of consumption sites like cafés and shopping districts (Graiouid 2007; Latham 2006; Laurier and Philo 2006). Similarly to affective practices, I consider these practices as embodied 'experiential con-suming' (Malbon 1999: 20) of leisure activities, through which consumption is a process and performance which transforms those engaged in it (1999: 29). These leisure mobilities from home to 'out' and back are part of what makes this holiday attractive as an activity and help it perpetuate year after year, as they transform how DVs embody their experience of Morocco. Their choices about leisure are as significant and important as choices about enacting root-edness. As I show in the vignettes that follow, DVs' choices about how they experience Morocco as a place for leisure consumption become intertwined with how they experience it as their ancestral home.

In particular, approaching leisure as an activity where being mobile is a constitutive part of the activity itself is one of the key insights from mobili-ties research that carries into this analysis. Rather than thinking of travel or transport as an inert activity – the 'nothing' that happens between places – this literature focuses on how moving is itself part of embodied and practiced human geographies (Cresswell and Merriman 2011). Engaging with mobili-ties research means recognizing how the habitualness of mobilities – like commuting back and forth between locations or returning again and again to the same holiday place – can contribute to how both the places and the jour-neys are experienced (Bissell 2010; Murray and Doughty 2016). It means appreciating how pursuing leisure is itself often a mobile practice, involving movement by vehicle (like cars, bikes, or trains) or on foot, or traveling to engage in leisure practices (Hui 2013; Rickly et al. 2017). It also means recog-nizing the politics of immobility as part of social life, in terms of who gets stuck, where, and why (Cresswell 2010). While the habits and movements of leisure are evident in the vignettes that follow, the politics of immobility are also particularly relevant when thinking about diasporicness. As (mostly) holders of European passports, the individuals I followed are able to freely cross borders between their homes in Europe and Morocco, while their fam-ily members in Morocco without those passports often cannot access the same fluid mobility (Mata-Codesal 2015).

All these aspects of mobilities ultimately point back to the ethnomethodo-logical problem I discussed earlier about what constitutes 'diasporicness.' If the individuals I observed are choosing to visit Morocco in part because it is a 'homeland,' they are also choosing to embark on the journey there in part because it is, for them, an habitual leisure mobility. Every part of the journey enters into the practices of 'diasporicness,' from organizing departure, to crossing through Europe and traversing the border, to traveling through and around Morocco, to returning home. By following along with participants during their journeys, I was able to observe how this set of mobilities is as much part of the way this group does 'diasporicness' as are ideas about *descent* and *place*. In short, visiting Morocco becomes a point where migra-tion and mobilities meet; where intersecting forces create a pull to Morocco that includes elements of tourism and leisure consumption as much as a search for one's roots; and a push of being a distinct generation who has ties and mobile access to elsewhere.

In this vein, I want to prompt research in migration to embrace a mobili-ties perspective in thinking about diasporic circulation and considering how it connects many practices in a mobilities spectrum. Diasporic visiting relates to the habitual practice of commuting in how, as I show in vignettes to follow, it is a collective endeavor and an annually expected event. It also relates to significant and singular encounters when ideas about one's migration history are solidified, and to leisure practices more characteristic of pleasure-seeking tourists. In considering this practice as connecting to multiple modes of mobility, I am trying to recategorize how it can be investigated by taking it on its own terms, as participants understand it, rather than defining it as part of migration.

Recognizing diasporic circulation as an ordinary mobility is one way this project embraces an ethnomethodological perspective. Taking this practice ethnomethodologically, as participants' own production of social order, is part of my effort to resolve the paradox of 'diasporicness.' Because it is a 'normal' activity for them, I treat it is 'normal' – as visiting home for summer vacation, just like any other family – and aim to investigate how it works and what kinds of social world it produces. Connecting ethnomethodology with assemblage, I consider this 'social' world to be vitally material as well – not just about what participants say and do, but also about how their bodies feel and respond, and how other objects and actors connect with them.

To do that, the vignettes that follow document both my own observations of participants' practices during their summer holidays, and conversations I had with them – held sometimes as formal interviews, and sometimes as informal chats – where they talk about their practices and explain their logics for their ordinary activities. I use a form of transcription following rules of conversation analysis (Hepburn and Bolden 2012; see "Guidance for Reading Transcripts" in this volume), which tries to reproduce how the conversations took place – including the stumbles, pauses, and interruptions – to show how these ideas were expressed in interaction, instead of as quotes isolated from context. The analysis I produce from all of this aims to understand how a social and material world is shaped through these practices: how their connections to Morocco are perpetuated and simultaneously reformulated; how their pathways through Morocco carve tracks that others follow; how the experience of visiting Morocco gets embedded in their skin, emotionally and materially. Through this analysis, I arrived at three forces that seem to govern the dynamics of how this assemblage moves: attachment, embodiment, and insulation.

iii Three forces in assemblage

The story of the holiday that starts in the following chapter is chronological, starting from the departure, concluding with the return home, and progressing through different phases of holiday experiences. Approaching it chronologically is one way to address it as an assemblage, where the actors and practices involved weave in and out of each other. Marking sections in the chronological story are vignettes that each show how forces of *attachment, embodiment,* and *insulation* act in concert to produce this journey of Moroccan-origin Europeans visiting Morocco for summer vacation. The pull of place and family becomes particularly strong through *attachments*, in discursive and enacted imaginings of the connectedness of descent. Physical and tangible ways of experiencing their environment, extending outwards to connect the flesh of a body to its surroundings and companions, manifest as *embodiments*. Finally, sticking together and keeping their distance from others are *insulations* that push this belonging into something recognizably, discretely 'diasporic.' Through exploring how these forces interlace and propel actors through a story of going 'home' over one composited summer, I analyze how *insha'allah* and *viscosity* reinforce each other and perpetuate the practice of going on holiday year after year.

Each vignette illustrates an aspect of a force through the practices and perspectives of diasporic visitors engaged in visiting Morocco for summer vacation. *Attachments* show, for example, how the journey to Morocco can be both attractive because of the chance to see family and distasteful because of the obligation to see family. *Embodiments* show how the experience of visiting Morocco can be internally felt as an embodied transformation of self, while also connecting externally by fusing one's body with other bodies. *Insulations* show how being a collective of diasporic visitors can generate a new community within a broader community by finding similarities among each other and contrasts with external others.

The summer holiday can be read from beginning to end (and back around to the beginning next year), or as separate interlocking parts related to each force. In addition, different elements in each vignette can connect to other vignettes, and are linked together so that the story could be read by following interconnections between elements.

By the time you will read this book, the story may be partially obsolete: new pathways have emerged, new sites have popped up, and some of the places described here have vanished since I was able to observe them during my original fieldwork. That said, while the specific locations have sometimes changed, the practices largely perpetuate. Though they may be interrupted by global events, diasporic visits – for this group, and for other groups around the world – will continue. My theory is that these three forces could be familiar to other diasporic groups visiting 'home' on holiday, though they may intersect differently through assemblages with other actors in them. Through my analysis, I believe that becoming diasporically Moroccan is congealing and focusing into an insulated *place* as leisure timespace, taking over certain elite pathways toward and within Morocco, as generations progress further and further away from Moroccanness as *descent*. Do you recognize these forces as relevant to diasporicness elsewhere?

References

Ahmed, S. (2000). *Strange encounters: Embodied others in post-coloniality*. London: Routledge.

Ali, N., and Holden, A. (2006). Post-colonial Pakistani mobilities: The embodiment of the "myth of return" in tourism. *Mobilities*, *1*(2), 217–42.

Anthias, F. (1998). Evaluating "diaspora": Beyond ethnicity? *Sociology*, *32*(3), 557–80.

Bissell, D. (2010). Passenger mobilities: Affective atmospheres and the sociality of public transport. *Environment and Planning D: Society and Space*, *28*(2), 270–89.

Brubaker, R. (2002). Ethnicity without groups. *European Journal of Sociology*, *43*(2), 163–89.

Chatterton, P., and R. Hollands. (2002). Theorising urban playscapes: Producing, regulating and consuming youthful nightlife city spaces. *Urban Studies*, *39*(1), 95–116.

Christou, A., and Mavroudi, E. (Eds.). (2016). *Dismantling diasporas: Rethinking the geographies of diasporic identity, connection and development*. London: Taylor & Francis.

Clifford, J. (1997). *Routes: Travel and translation in the late twentieth century*. Cambridge, MA: Harvard University Press.

Cohen, R. (1997). *Global diasporas*. London: UCL Press.

Coles, T., and Timothy, D.J. (2004). "My field is the world": Conceptualizing diasporas, travel and tourism. In Coles, T., and Timothy, D.J. (Eds.). *Tourism, diasporas and space*. London; New York: Routledge, 50–61.

Conway, D., and Potter, R.B. (2009). Return of the next generations: Transnational mobilities, family demographics and experiences, multi-local spaces. In Conway, D., and Potter, R.B. (Eds.). *Return migration of the next generations: 21st century transnational mobility*. Aldershot: Ashgate, 223–42.

Conway, D., Potter, R.B., and Bernard, G.S. (2009). Repetitive visiting as a pre-return transnational strategy among youthful Trinidadian returnees. *Mobilities*, *4*(2), 249–73.

Cresswell, T. (2010). Towards a politics of mobility. *Environment and Planning D: Society and Space*, *28*, 17–31.

Cresswell, T., and Merriman, P. (Eds.). (2011). *Geographies of mobilities: Practices, spaces, subjects*. Abingdon: Ashgate.

de Graincourt, M. (2010). *Leur Maroc. Regard d'écrivains, artistes, voyageurs, Venus d'ailleurs*. Casablanca: Malika; BMCI.

DeLanda, M. (2002). *Intensive science and virtual philosophy*. London: Continuum.
———. (2006). *A new philosophy of society: Assemblage theory and social complexity*. London: Continuum.
Duval, D.T. (2003). When hosts become guests: Return visits and diasporic identities in a Commonwealth eastern Caribbean community. *Current Issues in Tourism*, 6(4), 267–308.
———. (2004). Linking return visits and return migration among Commonwealth eastern Caribbean migrants in Toronto. *Global Networks*, 4(1), 51–67.
Gallan, B. (2015). Night lives: Heterotopia, youth transitions and cultural infrastructure in the urban night. *Urban Studies*, 52(3), 555–70.
Garfinkel, H. (1984). *Studies in ethnomethodology* (2nd ed.). Cambridge: Polity Press.
Gilroy, P. (1993). *The Black Atlantic: Modernity and double consciousness*. Cambridge, MA: Harvard University Press.
Glick Schiller, N. (2005). Blood and belonging: Long distance nationalism and the world beyond. In McKinnon, S., and Silverman, S. (Eds.). *Complexities beyond nature & nurture*. Chicago, IL: University of Chicago Press, 289–312.
Graiouid, S. (2007). A place on the terrace: Café culture and the public sphere in Morocco. *The Journal of North African Studies*, 12(4), 531–50.
Green, M. (1991). *The dream at the end of the world: Paul Bowles and the Literary Renegades in Tangier*. New York: Harper Collins.
Hepburn, A., and Bolden, G.B. (2012). The conversation analytic approach to transcription. In Sidness, J., and Stivers, T. (Eds.). *The handbook of conversation analysis*. John Wiley & Sons, Ltd., 57–76. https://doi.org/10.1002/9781118325001.ch4.
Hollinshead, K. (2004). Tourism and third space populations: The restless motion of diaspora peoples. In Coles, T., and Timothy, D.J. (Eds.). *Tourism, diasporas and space*. London; New York: Routledge, 50–61.
Hui, A. (2013). Moving with practices: The discontinuous, rhythmic and material mobilities of leisure. *Social & Cultural Geography*, 14(8), 888–908.
Jones, J.P., Woodward, K., and Marston, S.A. (2007). Situating flatness. *Transactions of the Institute of British Geographers*, 32(2), 264–76.
Kalra, V.S., Kaur, R., and Hutnyk, J. (2005). *Diaspora and hybridity, theory, culture & society*. London: Sage.
Katz, J. (1999). *How emotions work*. Chicago, IL; London: University of Chicago Press.
Katz, J., and Csordas, T.J. (2003). Phenomenological ethnography in sociology and anthropology. *Ethnography*, 4(3), 275–88.
Latham, A. (2006). Sociality and the cosmopolitan imagination: National, cosmopolitan and local imaginaries in Auckland, New Zealand. In Binnie, J., Holloway, J., Millington, S., and Young, C. (Eds.). *Cosmopolitan urbanism*. London: Routledge, 79–111.
Latham, A., and Wagner, L. (2021). Experiments in becoming: Corporeality, attunement and doing research. *Cultural Geographies*, 28(1), 91–108.
Laurier, E., and Philo, C. (2006). Possible geographies: A passing encounter in a café. *Area*, 38(4), 353–63.
Levitt, P. (2009). Roots and routes: Understanding the lives of the second generation transnationally. *Journal of Ethnic and Migration Studies*, 35(7), 1225–42.
Liberman, K. (2013). *More studies in ethnomethodology*. Albany: State University of New York Press.
Malbon, B. (1999). *Clubbing: Dancing, ecstasy and vitality*. London: Routledge.

Malkki, L. (1992). National Geographic: The rooting of peoples and the territorialization of national identity among scholars and refugees. *Cultural Anthropology*, 7(1), 24–44.

Massey, D. (2005). *For space*. London: Sage.

Mata-Codesal, D. (2015). Ways of staying put in Ecuador: Social and embodied experiences of mobility–immobility interactions. *Journal of Ethnic and Migration Studies*, 41(14), 2274–90.

Mavroudi, E. (2007). Diaspora as process: (De)constructing boundaries. *Geography Compass*, 1(3), 467–79.

Maynard, D.W., and Clayman, S.E. (1991). The diversity of ethnomethodology. *Annual Review of Sociology*, 17(1), 385–418.

Minca, C., and Oakes, T. (Eds.). (2006). *Travels in paradox: Remapping tourism*. Lanham, MD: Rowman & Littlefield Publishers.

Minca, C., and Wagner, L.B. (2016). *Moroccan dreams: Orientalist myth, colonial legacy*. London: I.B. Tauris.

Murray, L., and Doughty, K. (2016). Interdependent, imagined, and embodied mobilities in mobile social space: Disruptions in 'normality,' 'habit' and 'routine'. *Journal of Transport Geography*, 55, 72–82.

Nash, C. (2002). Genealogical Identities. *Environment and Planning D: Society and Space*, 20, 27–52.

Rickly, J., Hannam, K., and Mostafanezhad, M. (Eds.). (2017). *Tourism and leisure mobilities: Politics, work, and play*. Abingdon: Routledge.

Robles, J. (2020). A most remarkable fact, for all intents and purposes: The practical matter of categorical truths. In Smith, R.J., Fitzgerald, R., and Housley, W. (Eds.). *On Sacks: Methodology, materials, and inspirations*. Abingdon and New York: Routledge.

Saldanha, A. (2007). *Psychedelic white*. Minneapolis: University of Minnesota Press.

Sassen, S. (2013a). Before method: Analytic tactics to decipher the global—An argument and its responses, part I. *The Pluralist*, 8(3), 79–82.

———. (2013b). Before method: Analytic tactics to decipher the global—An argument and its responses, part II. *The Pluralist*, 8(3), 101–12.

Schnapper, D. (1999). From nation-state to the transnational world: On the meaning and usefulness of diaspora as a concept. *Diaspora*, 8(3), 225–55.

Shaw, R. (2014). Beyond night-time economy: Affective atmospheres of the urban night. *Geoforum*, 51, 87–95.

Shuval, J.T. (2000). Diaspora migration: Definitional ambiguities and a theoretical paradigm. *International Migration*, 38(5), 41–57.

Stafford, J., Bélanger, C.-E., and Sarrasin, B. (1996). *Développement et Tourisme Au Maroc*. Montréal: Harmattan.

Taussig, M. (1993). *Mimesis and alterity*. New York; London: Routledge.

Tölölyan, K. (1996). Rethinking diaspora(s): Stateless power in the transnational moment. *Diaspora*, 5(1), 3–37.

Wagner, L.B. (2012). Feeling diasporic (Paper No. 21). *Tilburg Papers in Cultural Studies*. Tilburg: Babylon Center for Studies of the Multicultural Society, Tilburg University.

Werbner, P. (2002). The place which is diaspora: Citizenship, religion and gender in the making of chaordic transnationalism. *Journal of Ethnic and Migration Studies*, 28(1), 119–33.

Wetherell, M. (2012). *Affect and emotion: A new social science understanding*. Los Angeles, CA; London: SAGE.

3 Vignettes

Attachments, embodiments, insulations

i Embodiments: Starting the journey

When does summer vacation begin: when you step out of the airplane at your destination, or step into it? Or even before that, when you start planning your trip?

To follow participants during the embodied practice of going on holiday in Morocco, I spent several weeks with Family B in Antwerp, Belgium (see "Appendix: Methodological Design") as some of their family members were preparing to make the summer journey. Luckily, I managed to join in one of the family cars to travel along with them. This vignette, and some that follow ("Embodiments: Crossing Borders," "Attachments: Touring Elsewhere"), document parts of that trip. It also shows how the embodied practices of going to and being in Morocco start to take shape long before arriving there; that planning and departing on this vacation is as much part of it as stepping out of the car (or plane) upon arrival.

Insha'allah departure

Figure 3.1 One of the children from Family B, ready to go. Antwerp. 11 July 2008, 9:30 pm.

DOI: 10.4324/9781003172383-3

Fieldnote extract 3.1 Narrative: Leaving Antwerp

Our car journey began in the small hours of the morning of Saturday 12 July, after spending the entire day of Friday on hold, prepared to go at anytime.

Negotiations were happening between brothers-in-law Brahim (post-migrant generation) and Abdelhakim (migrating generation) about when to begin the journey: Brahim was coordinating with his father as well, and in the end, our car (Abdelhakim's small four-door) is ready to depart with no sign of Brahim. We are awaiting news from Brahim outside Abdelhakim and Zohra's house, on a dark, otherwise silent neighborhood street in Antwerp.

Malika and I were delivered here by another cousin, and we manage to insert our bags into the car, whose trunk barely shuts already. Every foot-well is taken up with something: food supplies are on the seat between us, as well as pillows and sleeping bags; Zohra has a small cooler by her legs.

Abdelhakim and Zohra's children arrive and mill around with us, saying goodbye to their parents for the one or two months they will be gone. For various reasons – lack of funds, or new babies on the way – none of the children will be joining them in Morocco this year.

Brahim arrives after midnight to tell us his father's car had some last-minute maintenance problems, so they will not be ready until the following day. Souad was so exhausted from packing and taking care of the kids all day that she has crashed at home, while her children are in the car with their father, overexcited about the impending trip. Abdelhakim decides to leave without them, despite his concerns about the possibility of breaking down on the road. Having a group caravan is safer, but he seems exasperated with Brahim and his family; we have already delayed by a day for them. If we delay any longer, we risk being caught in the French traffic caused by the 14 July holiday weekend. Finally, after a week of waiting and uncertainty, we are on our way in the pitch black. Eventually I fall asleep, and wake up somewhere outside Paris.

The trope of *insha'allah* spontaneity associated with going to Morocco becomes part of our journey even before we depart from this Belgian home. Our departure finally happened through a series of uncertain events, with many entities adding their agency to the process: Abdelhakim and Brahim; Brahim's father and his car; Abdelhakim and Zohra's children gathered to see us off; and the impending traffic of the hundreds of thousands of cars not yet mobilized in France. Moroccan DV summer vacation consistently begins more or less this way, with progress, setbacks, and some uncertainty, but always Morocco as the objective.

Long before crossing the border, 'Moroccanness' as an assemblage becomes more materially present and experientially energetic, as participants move physically and affectively closer to the physical territory of Morocco. Still territorially in Europe, our car and its occupants were already primed for crossing over ("Embodiments: Crossing Borders") as we became part of the flow of other cars and passengers toward Morocco. We were sent off by family members, without our expected caravan, but still anticipating that we would join the collective of other diasporic Moroccan cars making the same journey along the roads through France and Spain, experiencing the same preparations, excitement, uncertainty, frustrations, and accidents as we did.

Conviviality on the road: Sharing stops, caravans, and problems

---

Fieldnote extract 3.2 Narrative: Rest stop in Spain

I don't remember much of France: we passed most of it by night, reaching Bordeaux by midday, and soon after the Spanish border. Abdelhakim drove nonstop, with only intermittent bathroom breaks and snacks, determinedly staying awake to reach our destination.

I wasn't sure what our destination was until we approached the outskirts of Madrid around nightfall, and Malika told me we were looking for the Moroccan exit. Once on the right road, we found it: a sign flashed by in Spanish and Arabic, "Area de descanso y informacion." It consisted of an open central area, ringed with picnic tables covered by overhangs and fluorescent lights, with a hundred or more cars parked orderly around.

The lot was effectively full when we arrived around 9:30 pm, but Malika's other brother-in-law Walid, who was traveling with his sister, her husband, and their two children, had saved us a place near their car. Although they had left Antwerp long before us, Abdelhakim's nonstop driving had enabled us to catch up. Now we had a caravan partner.

The rest area was minimally equipped: a bathroom with some shower facilities, and a drinks and snacks counter mostly staffed by Moroccans. I was noticeably a rare non-Moroccan visitor. We queued for the toilets (some of which were no longer working because of high demand) along with the other occupants for the night, who eyed each other and chatted in their own languages with their own families.

The single enclosed building, apart from the water facilities, seemed to be a police post that was locked to the general public; I looked in the window and saw a group of people playing cards, oblivious to the activity outside. We ate some french fries, sodas and coffee from the drinks stand, and settled into sleeping arrangements. We couldn't all recline in the car, so Malika and I took sleeping bags to a picnic table, while Zohra and Abdelhakim leaned their seats back. For midsummer, the night was remarkably cold; I was thankful Malika had thought to pack a sleeping bag for me. Sometime that night, a woman's car was robbed, we learned the next morning; there were some comments in the group about the safety of this rest area, which was safer than other places but still not protected.

Figure 3.2 Rest stop exit sign. Outside Madrid, Spain. 12 July 2008, 9:30 pm.

Figure 3.3 Parking at the 'Moroccan' rest area outside Madrid. 12 July 2008, 10:30 pm. The snack counter is the lit space in the background.

Figure 3.4 Bathroom door, 'Moroccan' rest area outside Madrid. 13 July 2008, 6:30 am. The graffiti includes numbers referring to French départements, along with some French city names and Moroccan city names, and normal claims and insults found in bathroom stalls.

Through the years of making this journey (more than 30 years for Abdelhakim and Zohra), drivers participate in and create systems for surviving the trip, and become familiar with landmarks, features, and problems of the route. All the drivers traveling from northern France, Belgium, or the Netherlands take roughly the same route, passing through Paris and/or Bordeaux, then near Bilbao, around Madrid, and toward Almeria. Although it is a transitory space, it is cohabited: one is aware of participating in a collective practice by recognizing other cars on the road, both known people and unknown people who are on the same trajectory (Bissell 2010). One stops for meals and notices other Moroccan families stopped at the same place, engaged in similar activities. In our interview conversation in Antwerp (25 March 2008), cousins Naim B and Otman B remembered their experiences of stopping at these 'Moroccan' places along the road:

Conversation 3.1 Roadside picnics

Naim B and Otman B, Antwerp, 25 March 2008, 30sec		
1	N	whe-when we wer- we were **young**, i-i-i- it took like **four days**, the cars they weren't like/ (.) **quick** like now/ (.4) and we had like eh/ (.4) every time when=we stopped, (.5) they made some **tea::**, and you had like a gas/ eh [how do you call it, eh=
2	O	[yeah (.8) and every parking there was a picnic=
3	LW	=eh xxx? like [yeah xx
4	N	[yeah, (.) yeah/ we=were every- (.8) had a picnic
5	O	=for- for an ho:[u:r or something f- (.) ahheheheheheh
6	N	[and they made [**food**, (.5) and they made **tagine**, they make **tea**
7	LW	[hhahahahah .hh hah .h hhyeah
8	O	so the picnic- e-::: [is
9	LW	[and you have to talk to everybody **arou::nd**, [and like yeah/ yeah.
10	N	[yea:h, of co[urse/
11	O	[yea:h, it was fun it was something al[l-
12	N	[every stop took like, (.) three hours.

In Conversation 3.1, the cousins describe how many families would be engaged in the same activities – cooking, sleeping, eating, chatting – creating temporary communities to be found and shared along their journey to Morocco. Importantly, this community happens in part, at least, because many families eschew commercial roadside services, like restaurants and hotels, in favor of bringing their own food to prepare (and sometimes cooking equipment) and sleeping in the car. The instigating reasons for this are economic practicalities, in that it is prohibitively expensive to feed and lodge a large family (a typical Moroccan family includes 2 to 11 children) on the road for multiple days. Moreover, halal food may be less available in roadside spaces with limited facilities.

While the time required for this journey has shortened with improved transit and infrastructure from four days to two, these habits of 'Moroccan' rest stops continue for many travelers. Moroccan families choose to stop in service stations that have outdoor areas where they can manage for themselves, rather than structures with plentiful restaurants and store chains. Even at the more resource-laden service areas, Moroccan families might be spotted cooking lunch next to their cars in the parking area. These practices keep Moroccan families collected together in visible places on the edge of the service area instead of mixed with the general patronage inside.

Figure 3.5 Picnicking families at a rest stop, northern Spain. 12 July 2008, 3:45 pm. We stopped at this rest area for a bathroom break. There was a restaurant and other facilities, which are in the opposite direction from the perspective of the photograph.

As much as these practices create a collective, cohabited space, they also illuminate how Moroccan travelers are separated from other flows of travel through these roads and service areas. They can experience difficulties in finding suitable food and in communicating with service staff as they pass from country to country, sometimes making them feel, according to some participants, unwelcome in transit. The existence of 'Moroccan' rest areas, like the one described earlier (Figure 3.5), is one way the physical presence of traveling diasporic families is sheltered, and they are helped along their journey. Places like these seem to be funded, at least in part, by the Moroccan government (according to signage on the few buildings there) as a service to returning migrants. They provide a physical location where Moroccans can fulfill their embodied needs: to cook outdoors, spend a night in the car, and especially to meet up with others in the caravan – both family members and other Moroccans on the same journey.

The existence of these sites reinforces the *viscosity* of diasporic travel toward Morocco by providing spaces where people meet in a 'natural' flow ("Attachments: Habitual Mobilities"). Yet accidental meetings and encounters fit the *insha'allah* of this timespace as fortuitous, or sometimes incurred by misfortune:

Fieldnote extract 3.3 Narrative: Unplanned stops in recognized sites

Malika explains to me that people favor the rest area just after a toll collection along the road, because everyone passes there. The specificity of toll stops makes it easier to know you've arrived at the right place, especially if you are trying to meet up with another car in your caravan.

We stop at one such parking area in Spain for lunch and so Abdelhakim can rest in the shade of a tree. During our hour there, I observe (at least) two other Moroccan families en route that have stopped here because of an emerging problem. As we eat at a picnic table, one French group – all young adults, not older parents or young children – parks not far from us, opens their doors, and turns on the radio. They seem to be in the middle of an argument: some of the occupants have departed for the toilets while the remaining two continue a heated discussion. They stay parked for a while, apparently waiting.

Shortly after that, an enormous white van parks farther down the lot. Eventually another car turns up to join them, but they don't depart right away. The respective back doors are opened, and things start being exchanged from one to another; it seems there is a mechanical issue, but I'm not sure with which vehicle. Abdelhakim finishes his nap, and we continue on before they are resolved.

The two vans that met each other just after the toll plaza demonstrate the practical reasons to caravan with other vehicles and families in case of mechanical breakdown. Though I could not determine which one had the problem, one vehicle was clearly in trouble and the other was on hand to help. Though each of the vehicles following our route, including ours, seems to be on its own trajectory, each is linked with others along the road. Part of the delay in our departure from Antwerp was because of Abdelhakim's preference to have a partner on the road. Knowing who else is before or behind you means that there is someone nearby to help a disabled vehicle, or at least be aware that one might be in trouble when you fail to reach the next checkpoint.

However, partnership can sometimes create more tension than it eases. While I was visiting with Amina during her holiday time in Morocco, she described the delays and annoyances created by her three-car caravan to get there, which included her parents and brother Simo, her aunt 'Khalt,' and cousin Sabah, and Sabah's sister, brother-in-law, and their children:

Fieldnote extract 3.4 Amina's family trip, 23 July 2008

last day in Hoceima with Amina

She tells me the story about their trip down, building off the problem of cousin Sabah being annoying:

Planning to leave Wednesday… Amina and her mom called Sabah and her mom (Khalt) to say be ready at our house at 6 pm. 7:30 passed, so they called to find out where they were; Khalt claims she's in Den Haag, with her other daughter, on their way (20–30 mins drive). 9 pm passes and still no sign; Amina's father says they should be in France by now.

Khalt finally shows up, Amina goes in the car with the 2 of them [Khalt and Sabah], all [three cars] driving until 7 am. After breakfast, trading off drivers to whoever is less tired, but Amina's father is driving straight thru. they make it to outside madrid, when Amina says they should stop to look for a hotel by 9 pm so they can find one with enough space for everyone in one place. They find a McDonald's with 2 hotels nearby; most of them eat, while Simo [Amina's brother] eats quickly and goes inside to check about rooms. the cheaper (€52) hotel is short a room, the more expensive (€66) hotel has enough, but the family with kids will have to pay extra, etc., etc. They seem ready to take the rooms, but then Sabah insists that she wants to eat too (after everyone else is finished), so they wait for her for a while. Then back to the hotel, where Sabah starts an uproar that they should just keep driving since there's only 3 hrs left (wrong) and that €66 is too much to pay for just a few hours. She convinces her brother-in-law, maybe [Amina says] by inflating the price to him, and against the wishes of Amina and her branch of the family, they keep driving.

An hour or so down the road, Simo sees a hotel and slides in before Sabah can say anything. He runs in, checks the prices, and declares that he will stay there, and Sabah can do whatever she wants.

Amina's story involves delays in appointments that create further delays, as well as clashes of will in leading the group and governing when, where, and for how long they might stop along the way. Abdelhakim was likewise frustrated by unreliable caravanning partners at our moment of departure, but relieved of his worry when we caught up with Walid and his family along the way.

Amina's example, however, hints at a generational shift. Each car has one or two migrating-generation parents along with at least two adult children. Although Amina was a passenger, her cousin Sabah was driving her own car, carrying her mother, sister, and brother-in-law. As post-migrant generation individuals become adults, they can exercise their own volition in determining the course of travel and how to participate in 'Moroccan' spaces along the road ("Attachments: Generational Mobilities between Morocco and Europe"). Their increased power in enacting the holiday journey will likely result in new roadside geographies of 'Moroccan' spaces for journeys. In this example, at minimum, the younger generation effected a stop at a hotel for a night instead of sleeping in the car – a marked difference from my experience in Abdelhakim's car.

Some troubles on the road have heavier consequences. A number of participants narrated vivid memories of frightening incidents, while others attested to knowing someone who had tragic experiences on this route. In their interview (2 February 2008), Family A discussed the memorable moment when 5-year-old Yasmine was left behind at a late-night bathroom stop: with so many passengers in the car, they did not count accurately in the dark. Her brother remembered their father driving in reverse on the highway to return for her. Jamila B (12 April 2008) remembered her experience at age 12 when her father fell asleep at the wheel early one morning while driving through Spain, and their car rolled in the ditch at the side of the road. Luckily, no one was seriously injured, and a passing car saw their wheels spinning and stopped to help. Others mentioned family and friends who had been killed in car accidents during the drive down.

These stories become part of the *viscosity* of the physical, practical experience of participating in the diasporic holiday. Perhaps traumatic incidents at the time, with distance they become anecdotes about the tense *insha'allah* excitement of going to Morocco and help to define the collectively recognizable experience of the journey. Sharing them helps produce a community of 'Moroccanness' in the holiday experience, materially extending Morocco's territoriality outside of its borders onto these cohabited roads.

ii Attachments: Generational mobilities between Morocco and Europe

The practice of visiting a diasporic home is one significant and potent manifestation of the force of attachment. As a mobility practice that requires some effort on the part of the visitor to enact it, it can express the importance one invests in family and rootedness. Yet, as a mobility practice, it is facilitated by mobilities of other actors – those who have preceded this generation and those who are enacting the same trajectory alongside one another. This vignette considers how practices of mobility between Morocco and Europe have coalesced into their current form.

Tracing backward, the mobility practice of summer holiday visits to Morocco by Moroccan families in Europe is embedded within several stages of migratory mobilities between Morocco and Europe. In the case of this study, the most relevant mobility was during the 'guestworker' migration period of 1963–74 (de Mas 1978), in which Moroccan men were recruited to work in European factories. Participants here are largely the children and grandchildren of those who migrated – only one or two generations removed from being born in Morocco themselves.

The migratory mobility of these guestworker men can be taken as a starting point for a whole series of mobilities that follow. Their partners and families followed them, and these families combined into vibrant spatial, cultural, and linguistic communities that can still be recognized as 'Moroccan' among the variety of diverse communities in Europe that have resulted from waves of migration (Daoud 2011). Many – but not all – of them reproduce habits and spaces that mark them as distinctively 'Moroccan' within and across several European states. Even in the third and fourth generations, Moroccan-descent individuals maintain some cohesion as a group amidst other groups (Lesthaeghe 2000). In some ways, through these communities, Morocco has become a space found in Europe as much as in the physical territory of Morocco (Wagner 2018).

Yet that is only one generational step backward in mobilities between Morocco and Europe. Stepping further back, we find mobilities of colonization

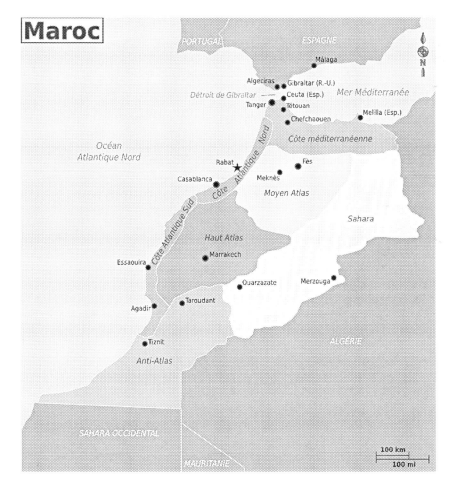

Map 3.1 Map of Morocco and its principal cities and regions. Cacahuate, French translation by Joelf, CC BY-SA 3.0, via Wikimedia Commons.

and empire, creating movement of many populations back and forth between territories, as well as mobilities of tourism and leisure. Tracing these histories indicates some control valves on mobility between Morocco and Europe – time periods and transitions when mobilities were forcibly blocked or made purposefully open, in both directions. Understanding how Morocco and Europe have balanced each other, as close neighbors across tense borders of cultural and religious difference, is part of understanding how Morocco has become a place where leisure tourism is accessible and desirable for its diasporic generations of Moroccans from Europe.

Generations of empire

In recent colonial memory, Morocco is widely known as part of the former French empire – as a protectorate for over 40 years, but not a 'colony' like its neighbors in North and West Africa. In fact, colonization by Moroccans in Europe predates colonizations by Europeans in Morocco, through the succession of Islamic rulers in the eighth and twelfth centuries (Cohen and Hahn 1966). As such, in the eighteenth and nineteenth centuries, Morocco was not immediately 'conquered' by European powers, like much of the rest of the world, but existed as an independently sovereign state. The Sultanate was seen by many European leaders as a place in need of organized reform and 'protection' (Cohen and Hahn 1966, 15).

That protection as an independent state was largely in the common interest of European global trade. Morocco's coastline, and its infamous sailors – a.k.a. Barbary Pirates – dominated the geographically sensitive site of a (European) 'global commons': the Mediterranean, opening through the Straits of Gibraltar into the passage to colonies across the Atlantic. Over the eighteenth, nineteenth, and into the twentieth centuries, a succession of Moroccan sultans maintained sovereignty and independence through this bargaining chip, especially as different European powers battled each other over territory elsewhere around the world. As opposed to a colony, Morocco was increasingly positioned as a trading partner.

During this period, the Sultanate likewise kept potential European occupiers at arm's length by controlling when, where, and how Europeans – whether diplomats or any other traveler – were able to enter Moroccan territory. This form of spatial control manifests in the city of Tangier, whose contemporary reputation for international mixture rests significantly in the century-long period when it was formally designated a city for diplomats (Stuart 1955). While the seats of Moroccan governance were, at that time, in Fez and Marrakech, foreign emissaries were limited to Tangier, where an international council of European embassies became the de facto municipal governing body. Effectively, even into the twentieth century, diplomats had difficulty gaining contact with the sultan without receiving his permission to travel to the interior (Landau 1952). At the beginning of the twentieth century, when many other colonial occupations around the world had long been in place, Moroccan sultans still maintained sovereign rule: Britain and France disputed trading rights with them, Spain continuously attacked the northern borders, and neighboring Algeria had been under French rule for 70 years (Pennell 2000).

During this period, Morocco became discursively enmeshed in the mysterious Orient of European explorers and travel writing. As it became increasingly surrounded by colonized neighbors, it became increasingly an object of curiosity, whose interior was blocked from view by the tight control of an independent sultan. Explorers of the late nineteenth century adopted disguises to travel through Morocco and avoid being recognized as Christian in this Islamic territory; they documented it as a land untouched by modernity and full of exotic peoples and picturesque vistas, in contrast to other places already 'ruined' by colonial influence (see Minca and Wagner 2016). Certainly, colonial goods were moving through the territory – including the British import of Indian gunpowder tea that is the basis for the ubiquitous Moroccan mint tea (Ennaji 2010) – but the movement of people was still relatively consistent with the long histories of migration within the sultanate and across Saharan territories. Nearing the turn of the twentieth century, when train travel had become the dominant mode of long-distance transportation in much of the world, Morocco was still traversed by animal or human power.

The transformation from independent sultanate to protectorate happened over several decades, interlacing Morocco's increasing indebtedness to colonial trade and the sultanate's close relationship with Algeria.[1] After several years of negotiating debts with France, Spain, and Britain and several near-misses at military occupation by the French, a sympathetic gesture by the Moroccan sultan toward rebels in French Algeria triggered new – this time successful – military action by France. The French 'protectorate' was officially installed in Morocco in 1912 under Résident-Général Lyautey, who maintained the sultan as effectively a puppet government for French empire. This French governance was not universal, nor definitive; land between the coast and the Rif mountains in the north and in the 'Western Sahara' was carved out as the Spanish protectorate, and French control over much of the southern *bled es-siba* (land of dissidence) took another 20 years to win.

Yet, having learned from his observations of Algeria, Lyautey's purposeful design of spatial planning in Morocco created opportunities for new mobilities of modernity there. Following his designs, the old cities were reified as 'traditional,' to the extent that modern technology was prohibited to enter (Wright 1991). New cities (often called literally *ville nouvelle*) were built next to them as places for French settlers – and tourists – to reside, with their gazes comfortably resting upon Moroccan 'tradition' at a distance in the old cities. This spatial design created purposeful division into two populations: a 'modern' Morocco of wide boulevards, galleries of commerce, and entrepreneurial *colons* (settlers from France and elsewhere in Europe) building cities with the newest available technologies; and a 'traditional' Morocco of narrow labyrinthine streets, artisanal handicrafts, and increasing overcrowding of domestic migrants attracted by the booming colonial economy but denied permission to use new technologies to remodel their neighborhoods (Abu-Lughod 1981).

Lyautey's strategy explicitly sought to entice both *colons* and tourists from Europe into Morocco, imagining the economic future of the territory to depend on the investment of new settlers and the preservation of its 'picturesqueness' – both in architectural and spatial materiality as well as in the 'traditional' peoples and way of life – as an object of consumption for the European traveler (Girard 2006).

These spatializing strategies are a colonial legacy in Morocco, and might be interpreted as a means through which imperial influence persists today. In being imagined as *touristic* more calculatedly and purposefully than some other colonized spaces, Moroccan landscapes continue to be made to fit a tourist's desire for 'tradition.' Discourses of preservation and authenticity pervade dialogues of tourism development in Morocco, whether with regard to its many different types of atmospheres proffered for tourist consumers across a mosaic of Moroccan spaces (Minca and Wagner 2016), or in the redevelopment of specific monuments as 'preserved' in the history of world heritage (Wagner and Minca 2014). Importantly for the mechanism of diasporic attachment, these purposeful machinations have made Morocco into a country that promotes, welcomes, and incentivizes tourism, and created spaces that DVs, in concert with their friends from their European homelands, seek to consume.

Generations of migration

In corollary to how it changed the landscape of Morocco, protectorate status expanded the potential for subjects of the Moroccan sultan to migrate beyond his territory. It enabled the circular routes of migration in Morocco to expand into Algeria and France itself (de Haas 2007), but not to the same extent that many other French colonial subjects came to settle in metropolitan France. Circulation patterns increased, establishing a Moroccan presence alongside other North Africans, but remained circular.

These flows did not turn unidirectional until after Independence in 1956, with the initiation of guestworker migration to Germany, Belgium, the Netherlands, and primarily France between 1963 and 1965. Though labor recruitment programs were initially characterized as temporary, they became bureaucratically solidified as the European states involved began to shut down the flow of recruitment in 1974. Disabling free passage between family at home and work abroad had the effect of making these settled rather than circular mobilities, and prompted efforts for Moroccan workers to bring their families to a new European place of residence (de Haas 2006, 46–47).

It also created new pathways of legal and illegal mobilities between Morocco and Europe for much of the 1980s and 1990s. Many existing European-Moroccan communities expanded through family relationships, while other communities, particularly in Spain and Italy, expanded because of their proximal accessibility across the Mediterranean and their burgeoning service and agricultural industries (Driessen 1998). These passages have become increasingly narrowed, as the requirements and restrictions placed on family reunification by different European states are progressively height-ened, and the patrolling of European borders becomes more and more lethal (de Haas and Vezzoli 2010). Geopolitically, Morocco has become a border zone, now acting as a European-financed blockage against African mobilities into Europe (Ferrer-Gallardo 2008).

The fusing of Moroccans into new communities in Europe has also enabled what might be seen as an intra-origin superdiversity (Arnaut 2012). While workers were often recruited from a single region to work at a single factory, creating European satellite communities of guestworker men, diasporic Moroccan-origin communities now broadly share many political struggles, with variations across European states. These include battling the negative effects of ethnicized stigmatization and underemployment[1] as well as problem-atization of differences in religious practice (Bistolfi and Zabbal 1995; Césari 1994). Some of these struggles parallel and intermingle with other migrant-origin groups sharing characteristics of discrimination or religious practice, like Algerians and Tunisians in France and Turkish communities in Belgium and the Netherlands, while all of them might depend on when and how different political issues become a battleground in each state.[2] Yet each of these groups can potentially consider itself separate from the rest, down to the original communities of guestworker men coming from the same village to work in the same factory. Across these differences, which may not be perceived by others, a superdiverse community of 'Moroccans from Europe' occasionally emerges – especially in the journey to Morocco over holiday periods ("Embodiments: Starting the Journey") – or is occasionally divided along issues like the shifting status of Amazigh culture and languages in Morocco (Aït Mous 2011).

Openings and closings

These shifts between enabling and restricting mobility between Morocco and Europe have contributed to the varieties of Moroccan communities now found in European territory, along with some of their diasporic mobilities as expressions of attachment to Morocco. While labor migration could have taken different trajectories – perpetuating as a circular process, for example – restrictions on mobility created the incentive for migrants to plant roots in their new homes, bring their families as permanent residents, and create a diasporic relationship to their Moroccan homeland. That diasporic relation-ship includes enabling the migration of others within family networks, as well as visiting 'home' once one's residency status enables borders to be crossed without concern. It likewise enables the diversity of people in Morocco to become one 'Moroccan' identity outside of its territorial borders, which is then reconfigured along different lines of sameness and difference in European political, cultural, and religious practices.

This variety of mobilities between Morocco and Europe has enabled two key factors as mechanisms of attachment. First, Morocco itself is a recog-nized destination for European tourists, complete with the transport and accommodation infrastructure that makes it an easily visitable place

("Embodiments: Diasporic, Touristic, Citizens"). Second, across many dispersed and diverse 'Moroccan' communities throughout Europe, those who can travel across the border and back often participate in the holiday journey 'home' ("Attachments: The Nostalgia of 'Home'").

iii Attachments: The nostalgia of 'home'

Fieldnote extract 3.5 Translated from a Facebook thread entitled Je bent een echte Marokkan als (you are a real Moroccan if), posted January 2010

You are genuinely Moroccan if you think back with nostalgia to those blissful times when you went up the beautiful Moroccan mountains with your family to visit the birthplace of your father or mother. The pure joy and welcome from friends, family and acquaintances is truly heartwarming. The peace, the simplicity and traditions make you realize how Western society has improved. Nevertheless, you cannot miss the other things!

Nostalgia for the past is a powerful component that fosters attachment. Undeniably, part of what some DVs seek in going to Morocco is a connection with *places* associated with their rootedness in Morocco, like the ancestral villages of their parents and grandparents. Yet, the sense of attachment that connects nostalgically to an ancestral home can be complicated. As in the quote in Fieldnote Extract 3.5, it can produce conflicting and simultaneous senses of distance and belonging. In practice, visiting other sites in Morocco beyond those that are specific and significant to one's own family can still express attachment as a connection to *descent*.

Practices of visiting nationally or culturally important sites resonate with generations beyond the migrant and post-migrant ones, as documented in work on roots or heritage tourism (Coleman and Eade 2004; Marschall 2017). Individuals who are many generations removed from a migration can be motivated to visit as a search for an 'authentic' connection to ancestors – effectively connecting to their imagination of *descent* – through experiencing a place of origin. For Irish-Americans, for example, Nash describes the embodying and performing of imagined connections of Irish ancestors as having, for many, "the religious intensity of a pilgrimage" (2008, 70). Yet, nostalgia often produces the imagination of an ideal and uncomplicated world, rather than one that actually existed.

> In some respects at least, settler genealogies of Old World ancestry reflect a nostalgia for an imagined time when place, identity, culture and ancestry coincided. Where you lived was where your ancestors had always

lived, and there was no dissonance between cultural identity and location. This is the ideal of bounded places, deep roots, and shared culture. The place of origin is the place where subjectivity is untroubled by the reflexivity of modernity and where collective identity is unselfconsciously lived.

(Nash 2008, 9–10)

The nostalgic ideal of boundedness, of course, does not hold up: for Nash's participants as well as mine, enactments of return become much more complex interactions of desires, motivations, expectations, fulfillments, and disappointments. The notion of attachment to a *place* based on genealogical *descent*, or an imagined rooted connection to it through family, inevitably is troubled by the unbounded complexity of lived experiences.

In the lived experiences of participants here, the parental or grandparental house is often a familiar reference point of the visit – a normal destination at the end of each annual journey. While that home can be an important site to visit, it may not always be the actual site that is visited. In the way DVs practice a dynamic of attachment, the diasporic 'home' that is an object of nostalgic desire can be more geographically diffuse than a house in a specific village; it can be the ancestral village or hometown, or the closest city, or even cultural or historic landmarks in cities elsewhere in Morocco. Rooted in their lived experiences, their decisions about where to visit incorporate access to resources, like time and money, and practical considerations, like convenience, as much as they are based in a nostalgic desire for 'home.'

Multi-sited familial 'home'

While most participants here spent a lot of time in the diasporic family home, often built by their fathers as a second home for summer vacation and retirement, their ancestral homes – in a parental village – may or may not be a regular site for family visits. For many, going to a family house is a multi-sited notion: a grandparental or ancestral home site might be in a more remote or rural location, while the diasporic home owned by their parents was in a nearby, more accessible town or city. Thus, going 'home,' in relation to familial connections, can mean the newly built house or the older one, each with its own associated memories and significances.

When I asked Otman B (Antwerp, 25 March 2008) about his experiences visiting family, his answer demonstrated this multi-part location of 'home.' He started by stating his preference:

I like to go to where- where eh: (.3) my pap- parents actually:: **came** from/ so/ up the mountains (.4) untouched by the: outside **wo:rld**, #(1.0) e:m:: cause m:- my father isn't eh: (.6) one of the city people. (1.3) like- (.7) he lives up eh: in the moun- eh: he **lived** there/

For him, this original village of his father was part of his 'traditional,' 'untouched' places in Morocco. When I asked if he goes to a family house there, he clarified:

> no um:: I went there- just- just to: be sure, hhhehh cause eh: (.7) just to let=you=know=I=mean, eh::m I just went there like ffhhhh/ two or three times, (1.2) and eh::: that's the::: thing that always (1.2) **stayed** with me/ so:: I tried to go:: the- this past year, but/ # it didn't work out/ so (1.0)
>
>   we stay- eh we stay there like just from morning to- to:: to evening/ [and then I went straight back home (.5)

Though it was long ago, the memories of visiting this place only a few times have stayed with him. But he hadn't recently stayed overnight there, only for a visit during a single day then returning 'home' – to his parents' diasporic house near Tetouan. In fact, visiting this place is not what he described as part of his 'typical day' in Morocco (see "Typical Young Men"). He continued,

> but eh:: just to see, like (.) eh::: (.7) with us it's just- (1.1) just in the:- like in the **old** days in- in- in the middle ages, like/ (.6) eh::: **tribes**, [like/ (.) this is the tribe from {name}, and this is a tribe, like the- the- eh: **those names** live **there**, [# so it's eh: q#uite (1.1) eh::m (1.0) **weird**, but- **fun** (.) to see tha- a- all that.
>
> [then my- my father gives a eh/ I live **there**, so/ and- and and- and::: we meet like eh (.4) **uncles**:: from my fa=hh=ther, (.3) ((smiling voice)) and uncle ́s **from** the un[cles, from my father, so::: it's the- it goes wa:::y back (.4)

Like other journeys to discover ancestral heritage, this one created connections for Otman between *descent* and the specific, identifiable *place* where his family comes from. It is not, however, a place he goes back to regularly. Most of his time is spent at the diasporic home his father built near Tetouan, in a relatively populated area compared to the rural, 'tribal' location he describes here. Yet his narrative elucidates ways that Otman traces his *descent* from this *place* through practices that he and his family repeat elsewhere in the world: their traditions come from the mountains.

Ancestral homes are not always sought out. For those who did make more regular visits to the rural ancestral home, the visit could be stressful and unpleasant, or profoundly boring. In contrast to Otman, Malika B recounted her impressions of visiting her mother's village as entirely negative: the journey was long and difficult because the village was unreachable by car, so the last part involved riding donkeys up a mountain. Her sister Jamila remembered being allergic to the mountains: the two youngest girls, Jamila and Malika, broke out into hives when they visited, which meant for them a faster return to the city and the nearby sea to calm the allergic reaction. In these circumstances, where the ancestral home is connected to experiences of suffering rather than tradition and rootedness, the idea of return becomes less nostalgic and less desirable.

'Home' in 'knowing the country'

Traveling to locate one's heritage can go far beyond the location of an ancestral family home. Almost all interviewees remembered their first tours to other sites and cities around Morocco as an important and exciting trip, in which they were able to explore and appreciate the history of Morocco more generally. Conversations about this tour were often framed by DVs as wanting to 'know my own country,' after having visited the family home almost exclusively. This sense of 'knowing' often meant visiting places in Morocco that are symbolically or historically important, like Fes or Marrakech – the same places that other European residents might visit ("Embodiments: Diasporic, Touristic, Citizens"). This pursuit is reminiscent of how national heritage tourism promotes belonging in the nation by fostering appreciating discourses of specific histories presented in specific sites (Light 2015).

Jamila B, for example, who normally visits her family in Tetouan and Tangier, told me she wanted to travel to Marrakech (The Hague, 12 April 2008). When I asked, "Why Marrakech?" she replied,

> because (1.0) I h- h- hear:/ about the the the **nice buildings**: and eh the **markets**: (.5) ther:e (2.3) and eh::: the **historic** about it, eh:: *Rabat ook, en Fes* {also Rabat, and Fes}. because it's- (.8) I think it's- it's my **roots** there, so I **have** to know how it (.) is there/

I commented,

> but- I=mean all of your family come from Tetouan, is it- (.3) do you feel- you f- still feel like Fes (.7) Fes and Marrakech are::- are part of your roots? (.5) are part of your history/

And she responded,

> n-no, but- Morocco is a **part** of my roots/ and (.6) Marrakech is: (.) a [part of it/ (.) of it. (.6) and I- (.4) I want to **like** (.) to go to the **south**, (.5) because I- always on the north, so eh/

Jamila's reflection represents how different locations can be part of her sense of 'roots' in Morocco. Likewise, others from the north who had been further south usually referred to that trip as a valued memory, or an experience in Morocco they would like to repeat. Rootedness in Morocco, according to Jamila and others, can be broadly interpreted to many sites that can be part of one's 'home,' beyond the familial or ancestral home ("Attachments: Touring Elsewhere").

Yasmine A, in contrast to Jamila, had traveled quite widely in Morocco (Wagner 2008). Her holiday habits reflect the flexibility of location in practices of going 'home': although she visits Morocco quite often – as many as three times a year – her visits to her family home in the deep south are less frequent, mostly because of its lack of accessibility.

Fieldnote extract 3.6 Marrakech or {Hometown}, 3 June 2008

Discussion at Café des Epices about choices on where to go: I was making the point that there's a difference between choosing to go to Marrakech (amusant, sortir, etc.) and choosing to visit family in {Hometown}; Yasmine says that going to {Hometown} with just 1 week would be too exhausting – it's not enough time (for the travel/distance involved). She's tired in Paris, she doesn't want to be tired on vacation.

However when she does have time, she spends more time with family than elsewhere – she gives example of last summer, where she was in {Hometown} for a week, then Meknes, then to Marrakech for the wedding.

Yasmine's perspective demonstrates how decisions about where to visit incorporate both emotional and affective factors, like attachment to family or memories of childhood visits, as well as practical considerations. The travel involved in reaching her parental hometown is more than Yasmine is able to do on a regular basis; she therefore spends more time elsewhere in Morocco, most often Marrakech but also at her parents' other home in another large city. In some sense, she expresses a strong sense of *descent* through her continued visiting, but, in her practices, the notion of 'rootedness' or 'returning to origins' is flexible. It can refer to an idea of 'Moroccanness' more generally, exclusive of seeing blood-related family in a stricter sense of *descent*. Where DVs go in order to be at 'home' in Morocco is not necessarily determined by *descent* as familial, but also through *descent* as a dispersed sense of *place*, embedded in many landscapes of Morocco.

Nostalgic 'home'

'Home' is, in these dialogues, a nebulous entity. It is sometimes nostalgically or authentically desirable and untouched, other times cumbersome and impractical to reach. For this generation, immediately after and accompanying the migrating generation on regular visits to Morocco, relatively few individuals have never visited their ancestral familial homes at all, as the site where important relatives, like grandparents, may still be living. The specific locations they might visit in order to experience a sense of attachment to Morocco, however, are not determined by or exclusive to this linear definition of *descent*.

As family homes decrease in affective importance – as elderly relatives diminish in number and family homes become more and more based in Europe – this generation's children may learn different habits of visiting Morocco, including visiting other *places* that are not so directly connected to individual ancestry ("Attachments: Perpetuating the Habit in the Next Generation"). Arguably, that does not mean their attachment is inauthentic; rather, it can stretch beyond the boundedness of nostalgia and its ideals of untouched *places* to stretch elsewhere around Morocco and incorporate other practices of visiting.

iv Embodiments: Diasporic, touristic, citizens

Many cities in Morocco have a message displayed prominently (in Arabic) on a hillside overlooking the population, carefully laid out in white stones: *allah, el waṭan, el malik*; God, country, king. These three words form one concept that defines the nation of Morocco as it has been imagined since Independence: a group of (Muslim) believers, embedded in this land, under a king whose power is undeniable through his religious birthright. All people belonging to this *place* – by *descent* – are considered part of that nation.

Unlike the European states where participants in this study grew up, citizenship in Morocco can only be passed by descent; having Moroccan citizenship, and belonging in the Moroccan 'nation,' is transmitted to any child of a Moroccan citizen, irrespective of birthplace.[3] It cannot be renounced, as is sometimes required to become a citizen of another state, nor can it be acquired, as citizenship can in most liberal democracies, by becoming a resident and meeting certain requirements for belonging to the nation. Moroccan nationality, in contrast with French, Belgian, or Dutch nationality, acts as an irrevocable and exclusive attribute of *descent* as much as a contract with the state.

Yet, even though DVs are all presumably Moroccan citizens by *descent*, their presence and activities as visitors bring up tensions in how they fit in this *place*. They may have attachments to the *place* as a homeland, but their modes of practicing their attachments sometimes align more clearly with leisure-consuming tourists than with ordinary residents. Moreover, these labels are operating simultaneously in their embodied experiences of Morocco: they are acting both as individuals pressured to be citizens ("Embodiments: Crossing Borders") and as people seeking to enjoy their holiday leisure ("Embodiments: Suntanning"). Rather than label them definitively as citizens or tourists, the tension between these two pressures shows another view on diasporicness in assemblage, in how DVs become touristic citizens.

Citizen tourists

Calling DVs 'tourists' is a delicate designation. McCabe (2005) argues that calling anyone 'tourist' has become increasingly problematic, as the term continues to acquire negative associations. It has become a contrast to one's own practices, where 'tourism' comes to describe a mode of superficial consumption as opposed to a speaker's own, somehow better, mode of behavior. Some kind of consumption is inevitable in any form of travel, or any contact with another place, as tourist, traveler, or even ethnographer (Galani-Moutafi 2000), whether or not the designation 'tourist' is a comfortable one.

Given their ambiguous sense of attachment, DVs are perhaps more sensitive to the implications of commodifying distance in touristic leisure consumption. Being assigned a label like 'tourist' implies that they seek what Zygmunt Bauman calls a 'pure relationship' with the place they visit, in that they have "no other purpose than the consumption of pleasurable sensation" (Franklin 2003, 208), completely divested of attachment beyond this act of consumption. Yet being called a 'tourist' is a label that materializes forcefully in this context, occasionally enunciated in my conversations with participants, both by DVs and by resident Moroccans.

According to Urry (1990) and Rojek (1993), structures of tourism have roots in bourgeois modernity and its divisions of labor and leisure. By inhabiting a work-oriented timespace, where labor efforts are paramount and concentrated, modern workers earn the privilege to inverse their activities in leisure timespace, where relaxation is paramount and concentrated. Mass tourism is one form of consumption that fills this leisure timespace, emerging from historical patterns of travel (Rojek 1993) as short-term consumption of an essentialized, 'authentic' experience of a place and its discursively-assigned attributes (MacCannell 1973). That act of consumption is embodied through exchange of economic capital – reserves of money and of time – for intangible, embodied capital, such as experiential enrichment, entertainment, or relaxation taking place at a distance from home. 'The four S's' – sun, sand, sea, and sex – have come to signify the major consumption activities that are codified as touristic leisure, to which Crick (1989) adds sights (places to see), servility (by others, to the tourist), and savings (comparably inexpensive goods and services) as part of the script (Crang 1997) of going on holiday. In short, as much as there are culturally prescribed ways of doing 'working,' there are ways of doing 'leisure' that fulfill expectations embedded in leisure timespace. These include the pursuit of appropriate experiences, including consumption of 'sun, sand, sea, sex, sights, servility, and savings' in another place, as ways one can validly enjoy being on holiday.

Between Europe and Morocco, relative access to specific kinds of capital is reflected in tourism flows and accessibilities. Thinking through DVs as 'tourists,' their access to capital procured by labor and turned into leisure emerges as vitally linked to *place*. Most workers in Europe have enough expendable income to invest in leisure spending that involves international travel. Places like Morocco, classified as "lower middle income" by the World Bank, are frequent choices for tourism from higher income nations because cost-of-living differentials and low-cost airline tickets make traveling there cheaper than traveling in one's home country. Resident Moroccans are considerably impeded in their international mobility due to visa regulations put in place by high-income nations. Such regulations demand proof of relatively substantial income, of job security, and that the applicant will not exceed his or her visa as a prerequisite for touristic travel. The flows of capital and tourists are thus predominantly unidirectional, of European tourists toward Morocco where the path is relatively free of bureaucratic and financial obstacles, and much more infrequently of Moroccan tourists toward Europe (cf. Stephenson 2006).

Leisure activities and spaces in Morocco geared toward foreign tourists, much like other similarly 'exotic' sites, are indicators of economic class among resident Moroccans who partake in them. Only those who earn salaries comparable to a median salary in a high-income nation – which in Morocco translates to upper middle class or above – can afford to consume these designated, exclusive leisure spaces. As would be typical in any society, privileged leisure spaces, and access to them, become more desirable and distinctive (Bourdieu 1984) as elite consumption. The differential access to leisure in Morocco emerges as parallel consumption environments, in which foreign tourists or those with access to 'foreign' levels of capital inhabit elite spaces, while local, domestic tourists, generally without access to those levels of capital, occupy more publicly accessible leisure outlets (Berriane and Popp 1999). As DVs intermingle with other leisure seekers in Morocco coming from 'foreign' places, they can become effectively elite consumers in comparison to their 'ordinary,' resident family members and peers (Wagner 2019).

Being elite consumers, diasporically

DVs' access to European capital gives them a choice as leisure consumers in Morocco: to participate in 'Moroccan' popular leisure spaces or, in parallel, elite 'tourist' consumption spaces. Their unquestioned access to these kinds of capital, which is often in stark contrast to their families who continue to reside in Morocco, cements the sense of class distinction between them and the majority of resident Moroccans. This distinction is echoed in research on DVs, who report perceptions of resentment by relatives or peers in the homeland because of their differential access to capital (Duval 2003; Potter and Phillips 2006). In many ways, their practices are identical to those of other foreign tourists: they follow a similarly structured summer holiday calendar and use their capital, both in money and in time ascribed to leisure activity, with the purpose of achieving the touristic affect of relaxation through consumption of sun, sand, sea, sex, sights, servility, and savings. DVs enter this dynamic as consumers whose activities mirror those of other foreign tourists, but who are also integrated into a locally-regulated gaze on their bodies and informed by their knowledge of Morocco as 'Moroccans.'

The idea of an exoticizing, subjectifying 'tourist gaze' (Urry 1990) by the consumer onto the 'local' is inverted for DVs. Instead of their gaze being 'dominant,' they are gazed upon as bodies considered, in some ways, to be members of the local community, yet transgressive of appropriate activities for individuals who come from their economic backgrounds. Although they come from primarily working-class families, often situated in rural areas, their accumulation of time and money as leisure capital – which seems normal in European terms – makes them stand out as economically mobile. Their class mobility, linked with migration from one or two generations previously, can seem remarkably fast and transformative (Conway and Potter 2009). While family members might be aware that they work in Europe, the majority of time they are present in Morocco is time 'on holiday,' trying to shed the feeling of a work timespace. They are engaged in the pursuit of beauty, relaxation, fun, excitement, adventure, pleasure, and sometimes knowledge of history or tradition that fulfills their desire for leisure capital accumulation in that timespace. As such, their choices on how to spend their labor capital to acquire leisure capital become sharply visible, socially relevant, and cogent to their relationship with locally resident Moroccans as a dimension of difference produced through consumption practices.

In short, DVs are acting both as citizens by *descent* and tourists in *place*. They are implicated simultaneously in discourses and practices about their belonging as part of a Moroccan nation and their behavior as repeat visitors in Morocco. In some sense, this dichotomy is a paradox that they encounter on a regular basis; yet over time, it is becoming normalized and integrated into the timespace of summer vacation in Morocco, in which the state welcomes back year after year its diasporic touristic citizens.

v Attachments: Habitual mobilities

Many members of diasporic communities are only able to make a diasporic 'return' infrequently, if at all. Returns can often be momentous occasions, like extensively organized family reunions (Ramirez et al. 2007), or once-in-a-lifetime visits to researched ancestral locations (Kelner 2010; Nash 2008; Reed 2014). Until relatively recently, migration on an intercontinental scale was predominantly a one-way trajectory, with little possibility for either temporary or permanent return mobilities (Berger and Mohr 1989). Yet some migrant groups develop regular patterns of return, which continue to be practiced by future generations (Conway and Potter 2009; King et al. 2014; Levitt and Waters 2002).

Because of factors like proximity, ease of mobility, and Morocco's orientation to tourism ("Attachments: Generational Mobilities between Morocco and Europe"), European Moroccans have a comparably easier time traveling to their ancestral homeland than other diasporic groups. Yet, perhaps more significantly, diasporic Europe-to-Morocco returns have become a habit: annually repeated as an ordinary part of the yearly cycle of family events. This habit invokes both a nostalgic sense of attachment to 'being Moroccan-from-Morocco' – to enacting one's role as a *descendant* – and an attachment with a community of Moroccans, both from Europe and from Morocco, formed by one's family and friends. This community is enacted, in part, by joining in the rhythmic, collective practice of departing for Morocco ("Embodiments: Starting the Journey"; "Embodiments: Crossing Borders"). Among the many factors that contribute to an individual choosing (or not) to participate in this practice, it is important to take into account how it is supported and perpetuated by social and formal institutions. Here, I look at how this collective habit is socially characterized as being part of a 'Moroccan' sense of spontaneity (*insha'allah*) and institutionally solidified as welcoming Moroccans from elsewhere into Morocco.

Pulled by the status quo

Though not all participants visited Morocco, those who did so usually went on a regular basis, annually or biannually, and were adamant about continuing to visit. For them, visiting was an assumed norm, not an exceptional circumstance; they might find it hard to imagine *not* visiting Morocco on a regular basis. As Zakia (Marrakech, 27 May 2008) described, it is an important habit she can't give up:

avant d'être marié, je venais **tout** les ans. (.5) il=y=avait pas une année où je venais **pa:s**, dès que je suis **née:**, je suis toujours- mes parents m'ont toujours ramené:, et=c'est=vrai=que =j'ai toujours:: <voulu> re:- revenir eh:/ (.5) c'est=quelque= chose=qu'il me fallait eh- voilà/ il me fallait mon départ au Maroc eh (.) à moins une mois et démi. et=c'est-t=vrai=que=là= dès=que=je suis mariée avec mon marie bon/ avec le travai:l et tout, (.6) on essaie d'y aller au moins tout les deux ans. (.4) l'année dernière j'ai accouché j'ai pas pu, donc=pour=ça qu'il y a deux ans, euh (.5) on était venu, (.4) et là cet année euh/ (.) je sais que j'allais=pas partir cet été, donc je me suis dit euh-/ (.) je vais venir une semaine et xx mon fils, (.6) mais euh:: (.) c'est=vrai=que=moi je- j'ai besoin de venir eh (.7) ça- ça reste mon pays natale.=fin pas m::::- je suis pas née ici, mais c'est mon pays, euh:: [(1.0) ouais

before being married, I came **every** year. (.5) there=wasn't=a year when I didn't **com:e**, since I was **bor:n**, I was always- my parents always brough:t me, and=it's=true=that=I've alway::s <wanted> to- to come back eh:/ (.5) it's=something=that=I must do eh- there you have it/ I must have my stay in Morocco eh (.) at least a month and half. and=it's=true= that=now=since=I've been married with my husband well/ with wor:k and everything, (.6) we try to come here at least every other year. (.4) last year I gave birth I couldn't, so=that's=why it's been two years, euh (.4) we had come, (.4) and now this year euh/ (.) I know that I=wouldn't depart this summer, so I said to myself euh-/ (.) I will go one week and abovexx my son, (.6) but euh:: (.) it's=true=that=for=me I- I need to come eh (.7) it- it's still my birthplace.=well not m::::- I wasn't born here, but it's my country, euh:: [(1.0) yeah

Zakia enthusiastically took up the habit of annual visits to her *place* (even if she wasn't born there) from her parents. Her perspective is just one example of how the habit of annual visits becomes socially institutionalized: perpetuated from one's family precedent, it can become the status quo of what is expected to happen every year, rather than the exceptional circumstance.

That perspective on the 'status quo' was reinforced to me during a dinner conversation (9 February 2008, France) with Yasmine A, her friend Saliha, Saliha's sister Nadia, and two male Algerian friends. When the conversation turned to the topic of my research, I asked about their visits to Morocco. Saliha goes back quite often to see family, and she, Yasmine, and the two men were planning a group trip to Marrakech in a few weeks. Her younger sister Nadia, the baby of their family, was looking forward to her planned trip that summer. "Once," Nadia says shaking her head, "I didn't go for two years. It was too much."

For each of these four women, going to Morocco is a necessary event, but with different purposes and constraints. Zakia, quoted earlier, was used to going every year, but her schedule changed with marriage and added responsibilities. Saliha and Yasmine, in their mid-30s like Zakia but unmarried, both visited sometimes multiple times in a year to see family and to travel with friends independently, away from the family home in Morocco. Nadia, in her early 20s, travels with her family to their home but frames the holiday as a source of relaxation time. Still, for each, it was a habitual status quo, without any end in sight.

While these visits are repeated and habitual for many DVs, they do not follow the same trajectory toward eventual permanence as their parents, many of whom own housing in Morocco as a precursor to an (intended) more permanent settlement after retirement (Schaeffer 2001). Rather, DV habits are about visiting as opposed to 'return.' They depend on the collective of family, friends, and community that visit together, making them temporary but reliable visitors, year after year. Participation in the annual habit of 'going to Morocco' becomes an institution that shifts along with changes in lifecycles, generations, and individual projects of diasporic Moroccans-by-descent. In some ways, it has come to be a characteristic element of attachment to Morocco as much by providing access to the place of Morocco as by congealing the diasporic population in Europe around the ritualistic, habitual mobility of visiting.

Habitual spontaneity

This sense of a necessary, invisible pull emerges as well in the way that traveling to Morocco happens as an unplanned but inevitable event. Every year, the time leading up to the summer vacation brings increasing activity around the question of who will go or not to Morocco this year – part of a pervasive sense of *insha'allah* ("Embodiments: Starting the Journey"). While not everyone travels, there is always someone around – a friend or a family member – who will travel. As decisions are made and reversed – who is going, who is not, who wants to travel in which car, who has to stay behind for which reason – the *insha'allah* excitement and anticipation about the holiday become part of a collective affect. The desire to visit mixes in with other forms of belonging, among family, friends, and a broader imagined community who are also, always, departing for Morocco around the same time of year.

The way *insha'allah* affectively works on who will or won't travel to Morocco is best illustrated in how Otman and I (Antwerp, 25 March 2008) discussed our plans to travel that year (Conversation 3.2 Insha'allah). At the time, I was trying to find a group to travel with during my fieldwork, and having a difficult time getting confirmation of who was going or if there would be space for me.

Conversation 3.2 Insha'allah

Naim B and Otman B, Antwerp, 25 March 2008, 30sec		
1	LW	um (.3) are you going this year? or do you kn[ow-
2	O	[inša'allah, inša'allah/ (.) inša'allah.
3	LW	°yeah° always right up to the day, righ=hhh=t, .h hheheh[ehheh (.3) who gets in the car and who doesn't
4	O	[yeah:: w- we don't- we don't plan e- yeah/ we don't plan thin- things like eh: that's eh difference between (.) **us** and (1.2) eh::: Europeans, lik#e (.8) they plan things, like/ **four five** months ahead, #(.8) we do that like/ two days befo=hhh=re=hh=we=hhh # (.) **go,** so::/
5	LW	yeah. I know/ this is my problem now tsseeh[hh
6	O	[yeah? hheheh[hh=
7	LW	[yeah. (.5) ye[ah
8	O	[=that's- but (1.8) **eventually** (.) those are the best eh::::::: vacations, [for me/ I mean like/ something that we do: on the **spot**#. then it begins like eh:: (.8) that's the best vacatio#n/ if we do something we plan ahead # (.7), then it do-::: it (.) it doesn't work out #/ no. doesn't work out.#

While Otman makes *insha'allah* something special to a Moroccan 'us,' in opposition to European holiday practices I was encountering this as a 'problem' because, already in March, I was looking for a family to travel with to Morocco. The sense of *insha'allah* spontaneity that made "the best vacation" for Otman was making my intended research trip difficult to plan. For him, it seemed like the lack of planning was necessary – otherwise, things would not work out. Even if it appears unpredictable, *insha'allah* becomes a dependable sense of what will happen every summer: traveling to Morocco will be reliably spontaneous.

Institutionalized mobility

As much as the spontaneous habit of driving to Morocco for summer vacation has become a social institution among families and diasporic communities in Europe, it has also developed formally through recognition by the Moroccan state, with tangible efforts to facilitate diasporic visitation. Both these institutionalizations combine to feed each other, making the holiday a perpetuating endeavor for members of diasporic communities and an increasingly important and recognized event for Morocco as a developing country ("Embodiments: Diasporic, Touristic, Citizens").

Multiple agencies of the Moroccan state have, as part of their domain, responsibilities of governing, monitoring, communicating with, and welcoming diasporic Moroccans. These include a number of institutions that have evolved in their purposes, since the former king, Hassan II, first created migrant associations as a means to monitor political unrest (Brand 2006). The most recently founded body, the *Conseil de la communauté marocaine à l'étranger* (Council of the Moroccan Community Abroad (CCME)) was organized in 2007 as a consortium between multiple ministries, concerned with promotion of the interests of Moroccan Nationals Resident Abroad (MNRA). The CCME mandate includes protection of diasporic citizens' rights while abroad, liaising with foreign governments, developing human capital, and "maintaining strong links with Moroccan identity, particularly in relation to language learning, religious education, and cultural activity" (CCME n.d.).

While CCME promotes transnational projects and linkages, the *Fondation Mohammed V pour la Solidarité* (Mohammed V Solidarity Foundation (FMV)), provides assistance to returning diasporic Moroccans, in coordination with the *Direction Générale de la Sûreté Nationale* (National Security Administration (DGSN)), as part of their annual *Opération Marhaba*, or 'Project Welcome' (FMV n.d.). The FMV orients toward various projects of public service, including aid to returning migrants. The services the FMV advertises to diasporic returnees include help in managing customs forms and roadside assistance on both sides of the border between Morocco and Europe. At the end of each summer, the FMV issues press releases with tabulations of entries recorded from the beginning of June to the end of August, sometimes broken up by port of entry, or mode of entry (boat versus airplane), that are regularly reported in national newspapers and dispersed on websites concerned with MNRA issues.

The national importance of these figures is also reflected in their reporting on the national televised evening news throughout the course of the summer. Alongside these figures, the news occasionally reports human-interest stories related to the in-flow and out-flow of *Opération Marhaba*, like road closures due to traffic or interviews with migrants who are happy or unhappy to be returning to Morocco.

The billboards and posters FMV displays throughout Morocco, as well as the television advertisements that play on the most popular Moroccan state-run channel, 2M, present narratives of families living abroad traveling 'home' to be welcomed by their families.[4] In these images, representatives from FMV are often aligned with family member roles, being helpful and welcoming caregivers to the returning migrants. Televised ads running in 2008 presented images of specific kinds of families participating in the return. In one example, two parents with two (young) children embarked from a neighborhood somewhere in Europe (probably France), pursued an uneventful journey (in ellipsis) toward Morocco, and arrived home across the border, into the waiting arms of their family. A similar ad depicted a family being greeted at the airport, with images of young children running into the arms of grandparent-aged adults.

Images like these contribute to circulating ideas about the return as oriented toward family reunion and migrant 'rootedness.' These widely dispersed, government-sponsored imaginations of the holiday present an 'ideal' visit: a smooth and unproblematic voyage, culminating in a joyful arrival to a welcoming family. The static advertisements interpolate the agents of FMV as the welcoming family, while the televised ads – which can be seen in

Morocco and globally on the satellite version of 2M – present recognizable alter egos of diasporic Moroccans who receive that kind of familial, familiar welcome associated with the idea of going 'home.'

Government-disseminated advertisements for diasporic familial attach-ment mix in with private-sector ones, like those for banks advertising easier ways to send money to one's family from abroad. One such ad, for a 'Kesma' bank card offered by Attijariwafabank, connected a younger man and older woman (maybe a mother and son) across the Mediterranean, as the "Bank of Moroccans without borders." Yet, like many advertisements, they do not necessarily reflect a grounded experience for the majority of their target audience. They present an idealized version of *descent* and *place* as unprob-lematically overlapping in the 'rootedness' of a family always ready to receive DVs (and their money). It fits with predominant notions of 'ethnic' or other rooted 'identities' that imagine concomitancy of *descent* and *place* as naturally unified elements. But as an image that is repeated and widely presented by actors with strong voices – like the Moroccan state and institu-tions such as banks – these idealized images support and perpetuate the diasporic practice of visiting by keeping it visible and present in public discourse.

Rhythms, habits, and institutions

Being pulled toward Morocco is supported and perpetuated in multiple ways. Some participants (though not all; see "Attachments: Resisting Pressure") expressed the 'need' to return, based in habits they perpetuated from their families. For some, the way this return happens as a spontaneous event is significant; it makes it a 'Moroccan' trip, unlike how 'Europeans' would do it. Ultimately, this trip is also characterized through the collective community making it together – whether that community lies in one's immediate family members all departing, or in the larger imagined community fostered by state institutions that have idealized the annual summer holiday as a way of expressing your rooted attachment to Morocco. As DVs are pushed and pulled toward Morocco, departing on the summer holiday becomes a way to 'be-Moroccan' in Europe, and also 'be-diasporic' as a welcomed family in Morocco.

vi Embodiments: Crossing borders

Traveling to any distant home involves crossing borders, whether they are internationally recognized lines (like that between Spain and Morocco) or borders perceived through other senses and affects – borders of time, space, memory, and belonging (Ahmed et al. 2003; Brah 1996; Massey 2005). The ethnographic fieldwork narrative that follows (3.7) describing the final piece of Family B's journey from Belgium to Tangier demonstrates some of the practices and encounters involved in finally crossing a legal and topographi-cal border to arrive in Morocco. This journey involved a caravan of cars,

Figure 3.6 Road sign in Spanish and Arabic at the exit for Algeciras, Spain.

alternately outpacing, waiting, and catching up with each other in the drive through France and Spain ("Embodiments: Starting the Journey"). As we approached the border, sites emerge at every step where 'diasporic Moroccaness' is embodied and practiced, both in the desire to return that brings all these families onto the road together, and in the practical negotiations – the paperwork, transport, and time spent – to finally cross from diasporic Morocco to territorial Morocco.

Along the Spanish highways past the southern coastal towns, our cohort of Morocco-bound traffic began to extricate itself from vacationers heading to the Spanish resorts. We become a flow of traffic toward the port of Algeciras. Through the congestion, highway exits, checkpoints, and waiting, each step is marked out as one step closer to Morocco.

Fieldnote extract 3.7 Narrative: Reaching the port

As we departed from Marbella, the excitement began to mount. Indicators flashed to us that Morocco was coming closer: road signs in Spanish and Arabic, so many other cars carrying the same load as ours. We fell into a deep traffic jam on the coastal motorway and tried to keep a lookout for Souad and Brahim's car, to stay close together as we approached the port. Some people pull away at Almeria to take the boat for Nador or Al Hoceima, but we are heading all the way for Algeciras. Once we clear the traffic jam, we stop together to buy our ferry tickets at one of the many resellers along the route.

Souad's kids are getting antsy and need to run around a bit without running into traffic. I help Abdelhakim fill in his landing card, Malika helps her sister with hers. When the tickets are settled, we resume the road.

It feels like we are at the port in no time, cruising on roads that are divided from normal city traffic to draw us straight into the boarding zone. You can see the enormous (empty) parking lot that once must have been full of families inching along in a day-long wait to board a ferry. Now the process is streamlined: we are herded into the ticketed vehicles for Tangier and queued in columns of other vehicles to wait our turn.

The wait drags on, and energy wanes. After two days of driving and sweating in the Spanish heat, I'm dying for a shower and a place to stretch out. I wander around the cars, trying to find new participants as we are all stuck waiting. I'm a bit surprised by the number of cars I see where the passengers are not a family, necessarily, but two or more adults. I bring back coffee for everyone who's still waiting in the car.

Figure 3.7 Buying ferry tickets along the road past Almeria and Marbella in southern Spain. 14 July 2008, 5 pm.

Figure 3.8 Waiting to pass through Spanish border control. Our car is behind
Brahim's father's and Brahim's car. 14 July 2008, 6 pm.

Figure 3.9 Queued cars, waiting for the ferry to empty. 14 July 2008, 7:30 pm.

While I was gone, Malika and Abdelhakim have obtained SIM cards from Meditel, the secondary Moroccan mobile provider, who are giving out free starter SIM packs to anyone who gives their identification details. They have distributors walking through the crowd of cars, and a desk set up on the side. I find a vendor and he gives me one after taking a digital photo of my passport. I'm ready to communicate in Morocco.

Eventually a ferry arrives and empties itself of a handful of freight trucks and even fewer cars. Everyone rushes back to their cars, so as to not miss the cue to begin boarding. Finally, our car is squeezed in amongst hundreds, on one of the multiple levels of car passage on that ferry.

Many participants described how, in years past, waiting in Algeciras for space on the ferry was a significant site of diasporic interaction, a pre-climactic moment on the journey toward Morocco. Participants remembered time spent in the parking lot queue at Algeciras with a sense of conviviality and hardship: setting up tents, cooking together, and meeting other DVs as they were sharing the traveling experience with the hundreds of other families waiting for a space on the boat. In some ways, it still is a site for interaction, though dramatic increases in the number of ferries and improvements to infrastructure for receiving passengers reduced the formerly day-long wait to a few hours. Now, physical separations have been effected between the immediate surroundings (Spain) and those specific actors temporarily cohabiting their journey to Morocco in the border zone of the port. We become people soon-to-arrive in Morocco, with the entrepreneurial move to provide us with communications (GSM SIM cards) so that we will be instantly enmeshed in Moroccan communication networks once we land.

Territorial threshold

Embodiment of 'Moroccanness' up to this point has been primarily a marker of difference along the road through Spain: while we might travel along with other cars full of Moroccans as a mobile community, we were passing through space that belongs to a different group. We could occupy a marginal piece of that space – at a service stop, sitting in picnic groups far from the restaurant that does not serve halal food; gathered in the non-serviced rest area where families park to spend the night on the edge of Madrid. Now, at the border crossing, we collect together in a zone of predominantly other Moroccans, ready to shift into embodiments, practices, and negotiations of belonging in territorial Morocco.

As a threshold, the ferry trip across the Mediterranean is also a space where the bureaucratic negotiations of embodied 'Moroccanness' increase in intensity. On the Algeciras–Tangier ferry, the official border crossing takes place during the journey: we board in Spain and arrive as approved to enter Morocco.

Fieldnote extract 3.8 Narrative: On the ferry

By the time we arrive in the passenger part of the boat, it's already starting to feel crowded. We find Souad and their mother, who have claimed a table as a home base for the kids. The men in our group have been dispatched to stand in the queues for entry control; there is one for passports and one for vehicles, and everything must be stamped before we disembark. The bureaucrats are of course horribly slow, but we arrive eventually to the head. There is a little discussion over the fact that Malika didn't bring her Moroccan national identity card, but they stamp her passport as a Belgian tourist and send her on.

Towards the end of our crossing, the bureaucrats processing vehicles abruptly left, with a queue of fifteen to twenty people still waiting. I'm still wandering around, looking for more survey participants as I hear the queue members realize their processors have disappeared and complain to each other.

On the boat, the environment feels 'Moroccan' and the rules of behavior are 'Moroccan,' including those for dealing with bureaucracy. Not having her Moroccan identity card has rendered Malika bureaucratically Belgian. While she was chastised briefly for not having it, others reported more intense harassment at the border crossing for not producing their Moroccan national identity cards. Said (9 February 2008), for example, described how he was sent to the back of the line for not having his Moroccan ID card, though his European passport was eventually accepted and stamped. Like many others, he interpreted this interaction as a challenge to his 'Moroccanness.'

The insistent requests for Moroccan-origin travelers to present a Moroccan identity card – even those who might be more than one generation removed – are linked to ideas of Moroccan citizenship as implicitly descent-based. In interactions like Malika's and Said's, an affective pressure is put on embodied practice: DVs are made to feel in the wrong for not having the card, and not manifesting a certain version of 'Moroccan' when arriving at the border.

Yet, these moments are also a bureaucratic problem of tracking entries. Everyone passing through Moroccan borders is tracked by a unique number. For Moroccan citizens, it is the national identity card number, which is used in many other bureaucratic circumstances. Border agents have been reported to accept expired national identity cards, as long as they show the identification number. Otherwise, the passport is stamped with a tourist number, just as any non-Moroccan visitor to Morocco would receive a unique number. In Malika's interaction, the border agents seemed to be trying to do their job effectively: to sort her as a 'citizen' or 'non-citizen,' by recording her unique, numbered Moroccanness. Requesting her ID card is one part of the bureaucratic process of counting entries in one category or another, for records of

Figure 3.10 Crowds and exhaustion on the ferry. 14 July 2008, 10:10 pm Spanish time, 11:10 pm Moroccan time.

tourists and MNRA that are then used across government agencies, while it also becomes an affective experience of embodying 'Moroccanness.' In the experience of these interactions, DVs come to link corruption and ineffi-ciency to Moroccan administrative tasks as part of what marks arrival at the Moroccan border.

Fieldnote extract 3.9 Narrative: Winding down

After dealing with the bureaucrats, we are free. The two children are wandering around, each with their own caregiver, to visit all parts of the ferry. Night is falling as we make our way across the strait, and I can feel the exhaustion of the road beginning to hit me, but there are no comfortable places to recline to be found; every space is occupied, the exhaustion is epidemic. Happily, we don't have far to go once we enter Tangier, unlike some cars that have a day or more of driving left before they reach home.

Nearly everyone on the ferry seems to be traveling as part of a large group, and each group has one or two small children to look after. There are no silent spaces: as I circle the decks repeatedly, I start run-ning into the same children circling in the other direction, sent away from their exhausted parents to burn off some of their excitement before we land.

Malika and I are on the top windy deck with her niece and nephew when we start to see the lights of Tangier become bright enough to seem like a city. By this time it is night, the sky is completely dark; I'm anxious to arrive somewhere, home, to relax.

The energetic atmosphere of the ferry as we arrived at the Tangier port reflects the excitement, and the tension, of finally crossing into territorial Morocco. Moving closer and closer to the border builds anticipation of being 'home,' but arrival there brings interactions that challenge the image of Morocco as a place of belonging. Surmounting bureaucratic obstacles is one part of this atmosphere, creating nervous tension as we creep ahead in the passport line. The exhaustion and frenetic energy of the noise and activity around the boat are another part. Both of these incorporate into an embodied experience of crossing over, showing how 'Moroccanness' is differently configured in assemblage as DVs transition from the road through Europe to the territory of Morocco itself.

vii Insulations: Familial obligations

Visiting friends and relatives is a self-evident motivation for many diasporic individuals to make a trip to their homeland. However, visits to family can become an obligation as much as a desire. While I witnessed many DVs visiting their extended family in Morocco, family visits can act to *insulate* them as a distinct and separate group as much as *attaching* them to Morocco as a homeland. Especially the expectations for visiting family – and their sense of obligation to do so – can act to insulate them, either by constraining them to spend time in certain places or prompting them to avoid those places and the familial contact they would require.

This sense of obligation has been found elsewhere in research on migration. One common manifestation of obligation is the expectation of material and economic reciprocity between diasporic family members and those who stayed behind. These expectations are often a source of frustration for returnees. Henry and Mohan (2003) and Mohan (2006) illustrate how a web of economic obligation can be embedded in the migratory project from the beginning, as migration journeys are funded as investments with expected returns and inherent obligations to care for remaining family. Visiting prompts those who invested to expect some form of repayment.

Along with that obligation, however, comes practices of avoidance. For example, Stephenson cites Khan's (1977) data on Mirpuri migrants in Bradford, who, in order to avoid the donations they were expected to make to family households, would stay in hotels during visits 'home' (Stephenson 2002, 414). While such demands for economic reciprocity might seem more applicable to the migrant generation themselves, they seem to extend into future generations. For both Stephenson's and my own participants, post-migrants experience pressure for economic contributions to familial households at 'home.'

These obligations also emerge in contexts of morality or culturally mandated respect. Velayutham and Wise (2005) discuss translocal enforcement of a moral economy, where failure to participate in practices of marriage or other social obligations by diaspora members engenders stigma in the home community. They identify 'second-generation' community members who experience pressure to conform to marriage practices of their village in the Tamil homeland, though the marriages might take place outside of that space (Wise and Velayutham 2008). Forces of attachment through reciprocity, in this case, are not exclusively economic, but involve respect for and adherence to practices of *descent*. Such forces of attachment may be countered by insulations in the ways DVs can make choices or take actions to limit – or even avoid altogether – the time they spend fulfilling familial obligations.

Limiting exposure

Obligatory forms of reciprocity and respect operate as agents that guide and sometimes limit DVs' autonomy in their choices of what to do while on holiday. Fatiha B's conversation about spending time with her resident Moroccan family illustrates how these obligations often can be unwelcome. As a single woman just past school age, Fatiha still joins her family regularly to travel to Morocco, but is old enough to largely determine her own daily activities during the holiday. Still, obligations toward her family are one of the ways her feeling of being on vacation can be interrupted, as she describes in Conversation 3.3:

Conversation 3.3 It's hard to be friendly

Fatiha B, Antwerp, 5 March 2008, 2mins		
1	LW	a lot of people I talk to complain about kind=of (.) the **pressure** to:- (.7 h) to::/ (.5) spend time with family there, (.) but you all- your family i[s here too so it xxx
2	F	[no. (.) so the- no:! um- we- if: my family from Belgium goes **there**, we would meet um: at the beach as well,=
3	LW	Mmm
4	F	=not t- to meet family, or we're not going- **we** don't go to Morocco to meet family/ we're going to Morocco just- because/ my father likes Morocco and, well/ we, (.) as well, .h um: (.6) but=no=not the pressure of meeting family, .hh um:: (1.3) but- (.) for=example if we would be at **home** and there's family sitting there, already, um:: (.6) it de**pends** on who it is. if it's family from Belgium or Holland, then they would go- go with us to the beach, (.) if it's family from Morocco, itself, then u:m: (.8) we would **hope** that they **won't** (.6) want to go with us! hh .hh ahhehh

5	LW	hh=why=hh?
6	F	ahhehh .h it's very annoying to- (.7) um (.3) like (.3) **socialize**, with people you don't (.) really want to **know**. ahhhehhh .hh I know it's a bit **mean**, but ahhehh .hh I'm not very intere-, I mean, you=know/=ok, it's **family**: an:d (.) but- I don't feel that- (.4) u:m (.7) that kind of **tie** like (.) I have with family, that lives **here** because I know them **better**, .h um:: (.8) but usually (.4) the people who come (.) to visit my grandfather are much older. hhehh .hh (.) sometimes they would bring their kids, but- (.) we would just (.) avoid them ahhehhhe [.hh
7	LW	[they are not interested in going to the beach anyways, [hehehehhe
8	F	[ahhhehhhehh .hh hh I would hope so=hhehh no but sometimes they just come to have their vacation as **well**, and that's a bit (.) **hard** because (.7) um:: (.3) you **could** do that a couple of times/ like invite them (.5 .h) u:m to go **with**=us to: a **vil**lage to have a drink or to eat/=
9	LW	mm hmm
10	F	=um: (.) but not **all** the time/ then you have to be **friendly** all the hh=time=hh .h and that's hh=**hard**=hhehh .hh especially if you don't know them,

Seeing family is not, Fatiha admits, one of her main goals in traveling to Morocco. She seems more enthusiastic about seeing her Belgian family (who live 'here,' in Antwerp where the interview took place) than her resident Moroccan family. Along those lines, she describes a context in which she is obligated to socialize with resident family: being in her diasporic home, with family sitting there – understood as locally resident family who has come to visit them. In that kind of context, she might be expected to be present, entertain and provide refreshments for guests, or take them along when she goes out (though she hopes they won't want to go). This applies to her especially as a daughter; elsewhere in this interview, she described her plans to go out being foiled by the arrival of relatives to greet her family, whereas her brother escaped these duties ("Insulations: A Typical Day"). Other DVs, particularly women, echoed these sentiments, both in terms of one's obligation to stay at home when relatives arrive and obligations to visit family members as an expression of love and respect. Given that many Moroccan families are large, making the effort to visit with all family members of equal status can be time- and energy-consuming.

As another example of unwelcome family obligations, Fatiha recounted in great detail an aunt whose continuous presence at her parents' diasporic home engendered both her annoyance and her pity. This older, unmarried aunt had had a very difficult life and survives as a ward of another uncle. When Fatiha's family comes to Morocco, she arrives at their house not long after they do and stays until Fatiha's father decides to return her home. She helps Fatiha's mother with housework – more voluntarily than her own daughters do – and takes care of Fatiha's grandmother, but she creates sticky social situations for Fatiha. Her aunt's presence becomes a constant obligation: either to invite her to go out with her and her sisters, which becomes an awkward outing, or to take care of her as an elder at home. Her presence is another part of what might limit Fatiha's mobility as she continues to practice the holiday as a family member in her parents' diasporic home.

As DVs get older and gain more autonomy in their holiday practices, they often become more able to evade the forms of familial obligation they do not want to participate in. This ability is linked to gendered household responsibilities. In opposition to Fatiha, a young, single woman who is expected to contribute to her mother's housework needs, Mounir is a mid-30s, single, French man who visited Morocco with an intention to see his immediate family, though he traveled separately from them. Mounir was accompanied by three friends on their month-long touring holiday in Morocco, who were planning their stops spontaneously (*insha'allah*) as they moved from city to city. In discussion with his friends about their next step, he interjected that he was due to visit his parents in his provincial hometown (Conversation 3.4 Comme ça c'est fait). The friends began an interaction negotiating Mounir's use of one of their two cars and the time he would spend at home with it:

Conversation 3.4 Comme ça c'est fait

Mounir, Farid and Omar, Fes, 28 July 2008, 40sec		
1	M	faut voir <avec> mon daron s'il a pas besoin de la voiture aussi/ c'est ça?
		I have to see with my pops if he doesn't need the car also/ is that it?
2	O	voilà, pis toi tu rentrerais avec le:: Scenic, pou:r trois quatre jours comme tu comptais faire, comme ça c'est fait et tu passeras [xx xx
		that's it, at worst you'll go back with the:: Scenic, fo:r three four days like you thought you would, like that it's done and you'll pass [xx xx
3	M	[tu vois
		[you see
		(4.3)
4	M	[[j'rappellerai mon père ce=soir (.9) **ah**?
		[[I'll remind my father t=night (.9) **ah**?
5	F	[[après c'est à part- ouais, si tu veux y aller, presque/
		[[after it's separat- yeah, if you want to go, almost/
		(.5)
6	M	hein?
		what?
7	F	[[ou tu restes
		[[or you stay
8	M	[[(v)oilà: mais en même temps **ouais**, je vais rester deux trois jours vers chez moi là-bas (v)oilà. comme ça c'est fait, tu vois?
		[[that's i:t but at the same time **yeah**, I will stay two three days at my house there there you go. like that it's done, you see?
		(5.8)

9	O	ouais si tu fait ça, c'est pour euh pas rater deux jours ici de=plus, quoi c'est tout (1.1) ici eh: tu [ferais
		yeah if you do that, it's for uh not losing two days more here, yeah that's all (1.1) here eh: you [will do
		[ah na- mais
10	M	comme ça au pire tu (v)ois je vais à Ksiba::, et comme ça c'est fait::, pis qu'après je peux bouger, voilà/
		[oh no- but this way at worst you=see I'll go to Ksiba::, and like that it's done::, at worst then after I can move around, there you go/

The way this conversation plays out, Mounir and his friends discuss the logistics of Mounir's passage to his parents' house so that it will provide the least interruption to their collective vacation. His friends make suggestions for scheduling and routes so that Mounir can get his visit 'done' and move on to meet them at their next destination, Marrakech. Mounir's conclusion to the topic, "like that it's done" (comme ça c'est fait) construes the family visit as a duty to complete so he can return to his own holiday movements.

Yet Mounir makes this concerted effort to visit his parents while on holiday. His visit is specifically to his parents – not his resident Moroccan family – whom he might also see in France during the year. His sense of obligation is entrenched in familial respect, but not necessarily including all of his extended resident family. Other DVs reported similarly that they are concerned with visiting Morocco out of respect to their parents. Sometimes seeing grandparents or specific favored older relatives was connected to this motivation, but often distance and unfamiliarity (like that described by Fatiha) had rendered these relationships less important. Instead, they practiced their familial attachments in similar ways to Fatiha and Mounir by using specific strategies to insulate themselves from those obligations.

In other words, seeing family is just one potential pleasure among others, but not necessarily a motivation on its own for this generation of DVs to travel to Morocco. For both Fatiha and Mounir, family is part of the holiday, but a limited part: purposefully limited or even avoided altogether so that they can be on the move and enjoy themselves. The desire to return involves precise calculations of benefits and detractions that incorporate elements of both family and leisure – of what can be tolerated in terms of family visits and what can be escaped ("Insulations: A Typical Day").

viii Attachments: Resisting pressure

Forms and expressions of attachment, as well as the sense of attachment to an ancestral home, will inevitably change over time. As Levitt (2002) found, these factors and dimensions shift through stages in the lifecycle, from youth to maturity, to marriage and parenthood, and so on. Though the choice to return is, for some DVs, an automatic and necessary act (see "Attachments: Habitual Mobilities"), for others it can be a tenuous one. They may resist going to Morocco altogether, or resist the sense of attachment that obligates them to spend that vacation visiting with family, preferring instead to pass their time in more self-directed leisure. As often as there are DVs who choose to visit because they want to see family members, or because they miss places in Morocco ("Attachments: The Nostalgia of 'Home'"), this section documents how others resist and complicate those pulls of attachment. They choose, as their personal circumstances shift, to visit without seeing family, or not to visit at all.

Yet, their resistance to the pressure to visit does not mean they reject an attachment to Morocco outright. Rather, all of these practices can be part of a dynamic of attachment that is flexible and malleable, waxing and waning over time, manifesting in different forms over different stages of life and in contact with different influences. This flexibility is what characterizes diasporic attachment as a dynamic force rather than a defining feature: it is one actor enmeshed with others, still present even when it may be fading or dormant.

Visiting without family

Mounir talked with his friends about familial visits as an obligation to be taken care of quickly ("Insulations: Familial Obligations"). Yet, his presence in Morocco demonstrates how a sense of attachment can still be enacted without being exclusively related to family. After discussing his obligation to visit family somewhat dismissively with his friends, later he expressed the feeling of necessity to return every year to Morocco. His form of return, in Conversation 3.5 however, does not prioritize family obligation:

Conversation 3.5 C'est obligé

Mounir, Fes, 28 July 2008, 2mins		
1	M	ouais quoi ce soit c'est les hôtels:, la piscine, donc eh: (1.2) fa niente, (1.8) repos/
		yeah whatever happens it's hotels:, the pool, so eh: (1.2) doing nothing, (1.8) rest/
		(2.1)
2	LW	mais c'est:- (.8) là c'est- c'est que ça pourquoi Maroc et pas:: [la Turquie
		but it's:- (.8) there it's- it's just that why Morocco and not:: [Turkey
3	M	_____[car Maroc c'est mon pays d'origine, [quoi.
		[cause Morocco is my homeland, [right
4	LW	_____[ouais voilà/(.) hehehhehhehe
		_____[yeah that's it/ (.) hehehhehhehe
5	M	comme=ça je=vois la famille au même temps
		like=that I=see the family at the same time
6	LW	Ouais
		Yeah
		(4.6)

7	LW	et il y a la possiblité d-m- au moins.
		and there's also the possibility o-l- at least.
8	M	xx ((wind noise))
9	LW	et il y a la- (.8) **possiblité**, au mois/ de voir la famille
		and there's the- (.8) **possibility** at least/ to see the family
10	M	ouais. (.8) la famille au Maroc il faut que je vienne une fois par an, c'est obligé euh (1.3) <si tu veux>
		yeah. (.8) the family in Morocco I have to come once a year, it's obligatory yeah (1.3) <if you like>
		(2.2)
11	M	même si je vais dans un autr- dans un autre pays, ou un truc comme ça, j'ai pas l'impression d'avoir été en vacances/ c'est quand je suis au Maroc que je suis dans mes vacances.
		even if I go to som- to some other country, or something like that, I don't have the feeling of having been on vacation/ it's when I'm in Morocco that I'm on my vacation.

Mounir frames his holiday habits as functional for both attachment and leisure: it is his *place* of origin; he enjoys the leisure aspects of his visits to Morocco; it's where he must go to feel like he was on vacation. Plus, being in Morocco means that he can see his family. In Mounir's case, family obligation can more easily be avoided or managed because he travels independently – with only friends, no spouse, no children, and no schedule ("Insulations: A Typical Day"). But being attached to Morocco, for him, is not intrinsically rooted in it as a *place* where he must carry out family visits. It is also about his enjoyment of it as a site to visit ("Embodiments: Diasporic, Touristic, Citizens").

Not visiting

In contrast with Mounir, Meryem B did not feel the need to visit every year. She was one of the few participants who did not have intentions to return in the near future. Her reasons, discussed in Conversation 3.6, are practical, and the inverse of Mounir: she would prefer to use her vacation for touristic exploration elsewhere ("Attachments: Touring Elsewhere") rather than returning to the same familiar sites in Morocco.

Conversation 3.6 Not going back

Meryem B, Antwerp, 9 April 2008, 2mins		
1	LW	what would bring you back to Morocco. like, what would convince you to:: (.9) to go visit again.=
2	M	Mhhhmhhh
3	LW	=anything?
4	M	I don't know actually/ (1.1) I haven't thought about that. (1.9) because I wasn't really planning=hh=on=hh=going back heh.[heh.heh.heh, hhhe
5	LW	[xxx, never again? (.) if you- like/ wo- do you think never again? I=mean/=

6	M	=no not **never** again, and=I=think,- (1.0) I don't **hate** Morocco/ or something but, (1.2) I don't really have the **need** (.) to go to Morocco/ because I have the same (.8) I think if you're going- if you're **having** a budget/ (.3) that you: (.5) want to **plan** in a vacation, (.6) you can: (.7) as well as go to another country/ (1.1) that's the- that's the feeling that have. so, (.5) I don't think it's **necessary** to give um (1.0 .h) ya- (.) like- to: (.9) go **first** to Morocco, because that's the **most** important (.7) I would say/ like (.) go and find yourself a cheap hotel in Spain and do the same thing!=
7	LW	Mmm
8	M	=be a tourist there, be=hhcause=hh it doesn't really matter, hh=so/
9	LW	um (.7) yeah, that's good- I mean/ (1.0) it's a fair point/
10	M	Yeah
11	LW	wu- u:m (.8) but it's interesting,- well/ some peo:ple:, (.) you=know (.5) u:m:/ (2.0) um, (4.3) like, sometimes there's a lot of **pressure** from: **parents** (.5) to: (.8) to: continue going to Morocco/ because that's, you=know/ it's- (.) it's something about your **history,** and/ (.4) where you're **from** and things like that/ but your parents they're not-
		(1.0)
12	M	well-
		(.8)
13	LW	well=I=guess- your father's there right now, isn't he so hheh hh hehheh heh.
14	M	um: (1.0) I don't- I don't think they would **pressure** me to go back, but p-(.) I think they would **prefer** it. I think that they wo- that they would be more **satisfied** if I would **choose** Morocco **above** another country. (.8) but for me, I would rather go to, I don't=know/ see **Italy,** (.) I've never been in Rome, hehehehehe I would like to see Rome heh.heh.heh .hh so:/ hhh
15	LW	fair enough,
16	M	instead of doing every time, the **same** thing/ with the **same** people/ in the **same** market, ahheh.

In that Meryem evidently does not feel the same sense of familial or *place*-based connection that compels others to continue to return, she judges the value of Morocco as a holiday destination, through the enjoyment or leisure she will gain from visiting. However, she does not disavow her 'Moroccanness' or feeling of connection to family and 'homeland' in Morocco. Rather, she questions her own need to go there instead of somewhere else that would be more interesting to her, even if her parents might prefer that she come to Morocco. In this sense, she values Morocco as a site to visit separately from its value as a *place* of attachment.

Losing the habit

Another part of this calculation is the force of habit. As much as repeat returns can become tedious, as they have for Meryem, they can become an inculcated habit, as they have for Mounir and for others ("Attachments: Habitual Mobilities"). Those habits may be particular to how 'diasporic Moroccanness' has configured for this generation, as I show in different ways throughout this book – the pull of family and community traveling together, the relative ease of mobility, the proximity between homes – but the habit can also be broken, or replaced by other ways of being 'diasporically Moroccan.'

I asked Said about visitation habits among his neighborhood cohort – DVs who were his neighbors both in France and in Morocco – and their tendencies to return. While he and his wife are committed to travel, he observed that once his friends pass five or seven years without visiting, the habit falls away. As he described it in Conversation 3.7:

Conversation 3.7 Let the thread drop

Said, Paris, 9 Feb 2008 1m20		
1	S	c'est fini, parce=que:: bah:: (.8) t'as l'impression que tu vas dans un endroit où tu connais plus per**sonne**, (.) les gens ont chan**gé**::, et tout, tu vas **plus** aller (.7 .h) alors que tu=te=**force** (.8) et là j'en connais un qui se force (.7) à y aller qu'ils essaient de s'arranger d'y aller **une semaine** dans l'année (.5) pour dire bonjour à la famille \<et revenir\> pour dire eh:: voilà quoi/ e:::o:: on existe toujours, quoi, (.4) et eh::: ceux qui arrivent à se forcer, bon ils y vont:: eh (.5) une fois euh/ par trois ans, par quatre ans,
		it's over, cause:: well:: (.8) you have the feeling that you go to a place where you don't know anyone anymore, (.) the people have changed::, and all, you won't go anymore (.7 .h) unless you force=yourself (.8) and then I know one who forces himself (.7) to go that they try to organize themselves to go one week in the year (.5) to say hello to the family \<and return\> to say eh:: there you go yeah/ e:::o:: we still exist, yeah, (.4) and eh::: those who manage to force themselves, well they go there:: eh (.5) one time uh/ every three years, four years,
2	LW	mm mm
3	S	et ceux qui, bah/ j'en connais dont un ça fait sept ans, dix ans, qu'ils y vont plus, et puis bah c'est fini, quoi. (.) il:: ils n'iront plus jamais.
		and those who, well/ I know of one it's been seven years, ten years, that they don't go anymore, and then well it's over, right. (.) he:: they don't go ever again.

Among Said's peers, he estimated 30% had 'let the thread drop' – had neglected the habit of return long enough to become disentangled from it. Said's description indicates how losing that thread perpetuates itself: once a habit develops of *not* visiting, the relationships and familiarity that motivated the visit can disappear. If the habit is not maintained, the *place* becomes more spatially and temporally distant.

This distancing can be part of ordinary changes in circumstance, especially related to significant lifecourse shifts. For example, Said went on to discuss another common cause to cease to return, citing his oldest brother who was married to a non-Moroccan-origin spouse. The dynamic of his household is therefore divided between visiting the Moroccan parents in France or in Morocco, and the French parents in France. Here, the thread of habit becomes entangled with other threads of influence that will make a difference for Said's brother, his spouse, and their children in how attachment to Morocco as a homeland is practiced ("Attachments: Perpetuating the Habit in the Next Generation").

Negotiating pressures

As DVs become adults with their own means of travel and multifaceted family connections, the decision to visit Morocco becomes a different negotiation. The pressure from one part of a family may outweigh the other; one spouse may feel more attached to certain households or places than the other; or an individual may seek other opportunities beyond the family holiday. Many members of couples discussed their compromises, such as alternating holiday years between the choice of a spouse who enjoys Morocco and one who doesn't, or making multiple visits in order to see one or the other spouse's family in Morocco. Often these negotiations incorporated considerations about being on holiday, and having adequate leisure during the holiday period, along with being at 'home' with family. They also take into account practicalities, like budgets available for holiday spending. In this sense, deciding whether or not to return to Morocco involves calculating the benefits or detriments of being in the *place* that is supposed to be 'home' against possibilities of going elsewhere for experiences not linked to 'home.'

As DVs transition through lifecycle stages, their attachments to family and to their Moroccan 'roots' shift, possibly leading them away from Morocco altogether, or eventually closer to it ("Attachments: The Nostalgia of 'Home'"). Mounir seems consistent in his habit of visiting, but this practice may change should his friends choose not to go with him or should he marry a non-Moroccan spouse. Meryem, who had no plans to visit Morocco, did in fact go the next year with a student group to do a tour of historical cities and sites – giving her a chance to tour new places while also being in Morocco. As intentions and desires to return fluctuate with other dimensions, visiting Morocco nevertheless remains an entrenched habit. Once the habit is formed, it may gain or lose momentum through communal forms as much as in individual practices of return throughout the lifecycle.

ix Insulations: A typical day

> **Fieldnote extract 3.10 Narrative: 23 July 2008**
>
> I'm leaving Al Hoceima very quickly after arriving, following Hind and Abdellatif who are driving down to Marrakech. I have invited Amina to accompany me there, but she can't – the possibility that she would

have to travel back by herself complicates the prospect of having a companion for the way down. She and I are saying goodbye at the bottom of the stairs, with my backpack strapped on ready to depart, and her brother Simo enters the house. It's the first time I've seen him in the three days I stayed there, since he seems to be always either sleeping or "out" somewhere, never materializing for meals or visiting grandparents. We say hello and goodbye in one breath as I navigate down the stairs with my bag and he starts climbing. I ask if he is going to make that trip he talked about last year, to take a car with his friends and get a bit further away from Hoceima than a day's drive, and he says yes, he and his cousin are planning a week-long tour, to begin any day now. His sister stops abruptly on the stairs, saying 'What?' as more of a statement than a question, with a serious look on her face. He immediately changes the subject, asking her for the keys to the upstairs room so he can go shower. After he climbs the stairs, she tells me this is the first she has heard of his plans; she doesn't think her parents know, nor does she think they will approve. But he, being a boy, will get to do what he wants, and she, as his older sister, will have to accommodate whatever inconvenience he might cause.

This fieldwork narrative of Amina and her brother Simo is a vignette of being on holiday in one's hometown. For most DVs, going 'home' to Morocco normally means going to the diasporic house – the home built by one's parents or a spouse's parents – not to Marrakech or some other city distant from the family. Being close to family, however, does not necessarily diminish the desire for leisure consumption. The activities both siblings pursued during the days I was there were much like those of any kind of touristic leisure consumer – going out, swimming, hanging out – but in a more familiar and familial setting.

For these siblings, going out in Al Hoceima often meant meeting or discovering their cousins hanging out in the same places, as much as it might mean finding friends they know from the Netherlands or other DVs they know from Morocco who return every year on the same holiday pattern ("Insulations: Viscous Places of Consumption"). Those activities contrast with their obligatory family engagements, like visiting older relatives who are still resident in Morocco ("Insulations: Familial Obligations"). Their participation in these different kinds of activities – as ways of demonstrating their attachment to family as well as their desire for *insha'allah* leisure – demonstrate how autonomy, often inflected by gender, plays a role in the insulated geographies through which DVs move around Morocco.

The conflagration of events retold in Fieldnote Extract 3.10 partially illustrates how a gendered inflection of autonomy works. Amina, the eldest sibling of five, finds herself superseded in travel plans by Simo, the second youngest. Whereas she was very tempted by the idea of traveling to Marrakech with me, she was not comfortable with the idea of returning on a bus by herself. Her prospect of a trip to Marrakech was impossible from any angle: even if she had a companion with whom to return, her parents would likely have objected to her traveling far from the diasporic household, to a destination unfamiliar to them, without a male escort.

Her brother, on the other hand, seemed to be anticipating a spontaneous car trip with his friends, one of the common ways I witnessed DV men exercising their autonomy in Morocco. As a man, even as one still resident in his parents' household, Simo is able to be more autonomous, as demonstrated by his *insha'allah* group trip, but also through his daily activities at the house. I observed during this visit, and a previous one in 2007, that Simo was rarely at home and difficult to locate even when he was needed or expected. In one instance, Amina left me at home one evening and went with her parents to visit her grandparents in a neighboring town. Simo was expected to accompany them but never appeared. As far as I know, no issue was made of this absence. His preference for *insha'allah* experiences over familial obligation was repeatedly made clear through his practices of being on holiday.

Dynamics that create an association between daughters and the home, family, and care are not at all uncommon in many global contexts (Blunt 2005; Conradson 2003; England 2010). In this case, Muslim-inflected cultural values reflecting the honor and shame of a family through its daughters (Abu-Lughod 1986; Aitchison et al. 2007; Freeman 2005) add to the intensity of pressure on women to be at home, and less autonomous. Traveling on holiday to a space of 'home' further creates an intersection between such gendered geographies of responsibility and moral propriety, and leisure geographies of pleasure and boredom. 'Going out' to any degree – out of the house, out of the town, out of the region – becomes a gendered practice demonstrating one's degree of autonomy by escaping the 'boredom' entrenched in the diasporic home ("Embodiments: Gendered Boredom").

To expand on how these dynamics of gender, mobility, and autonomous leisure intersect, this vignette reproduces extended conversations with three groups of young, (mostly) unmarried male and female participants of a typical day or normal activities in Morocco. Collectively, the stories reflect trends that I witnessed as a participant observer staying with DVs in family homes and illustrate tendencies about spending time with family in contrast to spending time 'out.' While everyone I spoke with professed the need or desire to see their families, how much time and how frequently they would visit family as well as how far they might travel away from their diasporic home varied significantly. Capacities, directions, and distances to which one can 'go out' can depend on factors like stage of life (in school/out of school, unmarried/married), how strict one's household was ("Insulations: Mentality and Distrust"), and configurations of siblings (e.g., if there is an older brother or male cousin available to 'chaperone'). Geographical trajectory was also important. For example, whether the family house was rural or urban, or whether it was near the coast or inland, might relate to both how easy it would be to access sites to 'go out' to, and to how safe parents might perceive of certain locations (see discussions about the beach in "Insulations: Viscous Places of Protection").

Gender, however, seemed more prominent than any other dimension in relation to a DV's autonomy while on holiday. It underpins these other factors, in that one's gender might significantly affect how another factor operated. Conversations 3.8 and 3.9 explore that from the perspectives of some 'typical' young men and young women, and one woman who illustrates how women pursue more autonomous mobilities (Conversation 3.10).

Typical young men

Conversation 3.8 Typical day 1

Naim and Otman, Antwerp, 24 March 2008, 6m30		
1	LW	what do you do on a typical day/
2	N	[[in the summer eh? in the summer.
3	O	[[typical day- eh
4	LW	yeah, in the summer.
5	N	ok: we::: wake up (.4) about eleven **o'clock**, (2.0) we have some **breakfast**, most of the time outside it- out**side**, (.3) not- not at home. .hh because we all eh **meet**, all the **nephews**, (.) we meet all with each other/ and then we go to:: [tras-
6	LW	[wait nephews or cousins?
7	O	[[friends
8	N	[[It's same no?
((4 turns excised defining nephew/cousin in English))		
9	N	then we eh: (.3) you know **the cousins** who live in Tangiers/ because we have a lot of cousins you know, who lives in **Tetouan**
10	LW	hhhhehh[heh
11	O	[so: #(.) #then#- #then- the cousins from **Tangiers**, (.) then go to have some **breakfast**, and then um: we go-=then we decide if we go to- to-/ the **beach**, (.) or we go to the:: (.5) to- just to the swimming pool, (2.0) and then we go to that place. and then we have- most of the time it's=the=beach, because swimming pool costs a lot, (.) it's about hundred and fifty dirhams/
12	LW	really? (.) wullah ((I swear))! hhheheh
13	O	ennhhh
14	N	and we go to the- (.4) most of the time to the beach, and then we swim/ and swim/ (.5) and fff you know/ (.4) **sometimes** we rent a jetski, or (.3 .h) if someone tha- that we know has a jetski, then we go with him. by the jetski/ is phh (.) but every day (.4 .h) that's it, and then we go **home** (1.0) and we arrive at home (.4) abou:t eh five o'clock, (.8) then we **eat**, (.) we take a **shower**, (.) we rest a little bit/ and then we go outside.
15	LW	so whe- when- **we** is- is you and your
16	N	cousins, [yeah

17	LW	[yeah ok. it's usually- it's usually all the guys together/ ri[ght? eh ok. and for you/ is it similar?
18	N	[yeah
19	O	it's about the sam::e, so:: (.5) I'll tell you the **first week**, (. h) the first week is just for family, so (.5)=
20	LW	yeah
21	O	=every day we go eh: (.6 .h) eh::- at the evening I mean, we will see family, so/ #(.) that's eh::: pretty:: much an im- **important thing** for us, in our culture,
22	LW	yeah
23	O	um: then it's about the same so/ in the morning (.) oftor ((breakfast)), (.)
24	LW	yeah
25	O	then I go to the beach,#
26	LW	do=you- do=you eat breakfast at home too?
27	O	at home/ at home/ yeah yeah. then we go to the **beach**, (.) we- we **first** look up the:: the guys from the **neighborhood**, cause eh: the family um (.5) in Tetouan, (.) all lives together, this- (.) it's **one place**/ so uh: then we go look up the guys from the neighborhood, and then we go to the beach, (.) about (.9) until six in the (.4) **evening**, then we go- (.) come **back**, (.5 .h) same thing **sho:wehhher** =
28	N	eat
29	O	= we take a:: hhhehh .hh we take a::: a:: a little nap, and then (.) go to the# center of (1.4) Martil. [not Tetouan:, (.) just outside of the- Martil or- o- or: Rincon Ndiq.
30	LW	[mm. yeah Martil. yeah I know Martil yeah. and those **café-**
31	O	[[and those café-
32	LW	[[so it's like you go on the boardwalk there? or like the **cafés** that are::
33	O	eh:: first the boardwalk, and then eh #**cafés**[, at the other #side of town, it's the same thing/ Rincon/ ehheheh .hh=
34	LW	[.hhh ahhahah
35	O	=so: (.6) that lasts about for **two weeks**#, and then/ (.) the plans come up. should we go to Fes, should we go eh:# to: to Rabat, (.) and then (.7) #for a few days we go out eh- **outside** of eh Tetouan or- (.6) #t-Tangier or some/
36	LW	to visit **them**? ((referring to Naim))
37	O	[[to visit them
38	N	[[yeah: (.) we go to: (.) [d-
39	O	[they do the same thing. (.) the beaches in Tetouan are (.) better than Tangier ahehehehe=
40	N	=yeah yea[h that's true (.) yeah
41	LW	[oh really, (.) ok .h hhheheheh
42	N	that's true
43	LW	but the pool in Tangier sounds like (.) ((whistle))
44	N	[[yeah but it's in a fancy hotel/ so that's not
45	O	[[yeah
46	LW	aww:: yeah.

47	N	you don't have-
48	LW	he- what kind of people do you see there/ is it other::/ like other Moroccan-/ ḥarij? or
49	N	yeah yeah yeah yeah, because they can pay it/ ah:, the people from Morocco who can pay that, they eh: (.4) you know (.5) th- they: (.3) they have a lot of money. [so/ [when we-
50	LW	[yeah
51	O	[the pool? I never went to a pool in hehehe=Morocco=hheh so
52	LW	really?
53	O	we have the beach, like eh: eh eh::
54	N	five minutes walk
55	O	r'oba' s'ah ((quarter hour))
56	LW	yeah
57	O	fifteen minutes from:- from home, so/ (.5) no need to go to a pool hhheh
		(1.6)
58	N	so/ (.) and in the **evening**, (.6) you know- you also want to know what w[e do in the evening?
59	LW	[yeah! yeah, (.) yeah yeah
60	N	ok/ in the evening, then we go **outside**, and then- (.4) we go drink something like a milkshake or I dunno. someth- **orange** juice, or a **tea**, and then we go to eat **again**,
61		((LW and E laughing))
62	N	[[and then eh no no
63	LW	[[sardines? or: (.) no. they don't have sardines in: [°Tangier°
64	N	[yeah they have, a lot. yeah of course (.) it's at the ocean, close to the ocean. (.h) ah:::::::m and then- in the evening then- we sti- we **talk** and um (.) we meet other **friends** from (.4) from Belgium/ also we meet there and then/ (.h) ah:m- it's just a coincidence but it's always the **same place** where/ everybody from ḥarij go, from Holland, France, (.9) ah:: (.8) you know/ we **all meet** at **one place** in Tangiers,
65	LW	mm
66	N	(.) and then we go **out** to a **club**, (1.8) if we don't go out to a- and then we go out to a club,- **if** we go out to a club, then (.4) we stay until the **morning**, and then (.5) **sometimes** we go immediately to the **beach**, and then we sleep (.6) under the **sun**, or/ we go first home and the we go. (.6 .h) but if we go- if we- if we **don't go** to a **club**, because we're not all- every day go to a club/ then we go (.)you=know/ **just driving around**, sometimes we arrive in (.4) **Casablanca**, (.) all of the sudden, (.7) or in **Rabat**, during the night, [you're just **driv**ing
67	LW	[has a- hhahahah
68	N	yeah we do it just **driv**ing, we- we did it ah (.3) two years ago. (.6) me and two cousins, (.) and a friend of us, (.) me/ my cousin [name] and [name] and frie- (.) and then we just drive around, and sometimes we arrive in **Meknes** or in (.5) **Casablanca**, or in **Rabat**, we just drive around.=
69	O	=we don't- we don't plan things, [[(.) like, weeks before

70	LW	[ye[ah
71	N	[we don't plan
72	LW	Yeah
73	O	it's eh at the sa- eh at the be-#
74	LW	Yeah
75	O	so[:::: same day.
76	N	[but the- then we forget- then we forgot- if whe- when we **start,** the- the the **trip,** then we forget a lot of things/ like (.) we don't- take our swim: you know/=
77	LW	Hhyeah
78	N	=our short =with=u (.) so we cannot swim if we arrive at the **p**lace so/ (.) or we just drive around until we arrive at Casa**blanca,** and then at five o'clock then we just (.) dr: there we just drive back
79	LW	Mm
80	N	because then, we think, like °oh shit (.) we don't have any° **shorts** or so[mething to **swim tomorrow,** [so/ (.) then we go back to Tangiers
81	O	[ehhehehehehe
82	LW	[.hhhhahhaha

As Naim and Otman describe in Conversation 3.8, nearly everything they do on a normal day in Morocco is oriented toward an *insha'allah* leisure time-space. These men and their peer-aged cousins are free to wander the spaces they have the mobility to access ("Embodiments: Having a Car"; "Insulations: Hypermobile Viscosity"). They are aware that their mobility is enabled by capital that exceeds the average Moroccan, as evidenced by Naim's comment about the expensive hotel pool (11–12 and 48–49), though they must budget their spending among a variety of leisure activities ("Insulations: Viscous Places of Consumption").

In contrast to the complaints of some women (see Conversation 3.9), the autonomous mobility of men is not constrained by family commitments or household work; they only come 'home' (to their parents' homes) when it is necessary to change clothes, take a shower, or seek shelter. They can limit their participation in family obligations to the time they want to spend on it. Naim does not discuss spending time with his resident Moroccan family at all (5–16), while Otman describes the first week as reserved for family that live close to their diasporic home (19–21 and 27), but the remainder of the month as leisure ("Insulations: Familial Obligations").

On leisure-oriented days they describe a routine between outdoor leisure, rest, and nighttime consumption activities regulated by *insha'allah*. Their program is both predictable and unplanned, only orchestrated through fortuitous coincidence and serendipitous encounters that turn into autonomous mobile leisure activities (62–82). The holiday becomes, in opposition to their work life in Belgium, a timespace that is profoundly spontaneous and relatively without limitations ("Habitual Spontaneity").

Typical young women

Shirin and Anissa's dialogue in Conversation 3.9 on their holiday habits provides both parallels and contrasts to Naim and Otman's accounts. They are in their early 20s and unmarried, and like the men, they each go 'home' to different places – Anissa to central Morocco and Shirin to the east coast. Their first consideration in recalling their holiday behavior, however, relates to familial and gender structures.

Conversation 3.9 Typical day II

		Anissa and Shirin, Den Haag, 10 April 2008, 3m30
1	LW	what for you was like a **typ**ical day (.) in Morocco/ (.) like (.) wake up early, wake up la:te/ wha- what is a normal day
2	S	ya wake- wake up eh:: not la- not too **late** but not too **early**, um:: eight o'clock, nine o'clock
3	A	do=you mean a family day or a day when we go:: [to the beach, or/ you know
4	S	[out yeahhahah
5	LW	either one, like,
6	A	cause a **family** day- eh- I would wake up early, (.4) because we would stay in a big house where all my relatives are, (.4) and then we would- eh- wake up in the morning, because eh/ in Beni Mellal it's very hot, you know=you can't sleep until ten o'clock or something like that, (.h) and eh:: we all have breakfast together, (1.4) and then what do we do/ we go to **family**! (.5) like/ in other ehm:: streets and stuff that, and um: (.4) go to the marketplace or- or whatever and then u:m um
7	LW	Beni Mell[al doesn't really hav:e a **beach** or a sw- anything to
8	A	[have eh:
9	A	no! it's very, it's yeah/ (.6) it's in the center of Morocco y=know, (.) no beach. aheheheh nothing! like you have a: swimming pool, [but/ (.4) we hardly ever go there
10	S	[ahehehe **one** swimming?
11	A	*ja ja blijf **één**. yeah. yeah. maar em::* ya ya there's **one**. but
12	LW	is it very expensive? or (.6) [a public/ is it like a municipal-
13	A	[no:: (.9) it's- (.4) °it's not expensive/ no no°. and then in the afternoon eh: (.4) we take a::- a:: (.) **siesta** ahehehehe.hh a big one, (.6) and u::m: (1.3) then we all have **lunch**, and then/ yeah, (.4) you=know=just- a lot of talking I guess
		((question about talking, 2 turns excised))
14	LW	LW: and for you, is that (.4) about the sa-
15	S	yeah, we wake up, yeah/ we=uh::: we go to the beach in **Temera**, it's near Rabat, and eh::/ (.) or I take the car/ (.5) when I had my driving license it was **better**, because I can take the car, and go to um: (.5) ah **Bouznika** or **Mohammedia** it's near Casablanca, (.4) t- yeah/ an::d then: (.) just for a day and then we come back but (.8) em:: my mom never lets us- (.) let us go to Casablanca alone/ because Casablanca is eh/ **ya**

16	A	[[ruwina, ruwina ((chaos, chaos)) ahhheheheh
17	S	[[a hard city ya <u>ruwina</u> ((chaos)) ya so she says/ **theddek** Bouznika ((**until** Bouznika))[ahahahahah and **theddek** Kenitra ((**until** Kenitra))/ I don't like Kenitra as well, so it's
		just Rabat, that's why I like Rabat,=because it's very **calm** and **cool**, no one=
18	A	[aheheheheh
19	LW	mmm
20	S	=**speak to you** or is eh (.9) so eh ya, it's Bouznika and Rabat, just in Rabat/ you go to the **city** and in the evening we go to **Temara**, with **family:**, my dad/ and my mom/ and everyone (.) we sit there, and we eat something
21	LW	so- so for **you**, like a day near the beach, like in Jadida, same kind of thing? you wake up and go to beach? or
22	A	eh:: (.) ya.
		(2.6)
23	S	yeah
24	A	probably yeah,
		(1.7)
25	LW	um: (1.0) so
26	S	it's real- just a normal day if we have nothing to do, otherwise we go with the- whole family to Marrake:ch, or [we, we stay for four days,=
27	A	[yeah! you have like (.) family trips
28	S	=or we go to Ifrane () I saw a lot of Morocco with my parents.

Whereas Otman emphasized the importance of spending time with his family only for the first week, Anissa describes her typical day as a 'family day,' in which she stays home or visits other nearby family homes in her hometown in central Morocco (3–6). Anissa's relatively small circle of mobility may be related to the lack of leisure outlets in her town. In order to go to the beach, she had established previously in the interview, she and her family go to an uncle's house in El Jadida on the Atlantic coast (21–24). Shirin's hometown of Rabat, like Tangier and Tetouan, gives access to several beaches, which she explored more fully once she gained use of the family car (15). Yet her mobility is still circumscribed by her parents: her mother warns her how far she is allowed to go, and not to go to Casablanca unaccompanied (15–19).

As young, relatively unburdened men (Naim had married shortly before this interview), neither Naim B nor Otman B is subject to familial or gender constraints. As their family homes are near recognized leisure spaces in the big city (Tangier) and a semi-rural countryside, along the northern coast near Tetouan, a typical day for each of them involves multiple forms of collective leisure consumption, reflective of their economic position as DVs in Morocco. Their geographical and gender positioning gives them (and their cohort of presumably male cousins) access to beaches, nightclubs, and swimming pools near them, but also movement around Morocco to other leisure sites.

The women do many of the same things the men do, but with familial companions, like parents, siblings, and siblings-in-law and probably their young nieces and nephews. Shirin describes her evenings like Otman, in that she goes to a slightly distant beach, Temara, which is comparable to Martil, but she does so with her parents. Anissa mentions at the end of this excerpt, and later described in detail, 'family trips' around Morocco in which she traveled with her parents or with a sister and her husband. For both women, there is a normal day with 'nothing to do' and days when they go away from the house, either out of town completely (to Marrakech) or to the local (or semi-distant) beach (26–28). Their travel, however, is not the profoundly spontaneous, autonomous, *insha'allah* travel of their male counterparts, as they practice mobility along with their parents.

While many women become more autonomous in their leisure choices when they marry, many young unmarried women are frustrated in their desires for autonomous mobility – like Amina's disappointment (at the start of this vignette) at not being able to visit Marrakech. Several women were exceptions to this standard and had traveled without parents or a husband, like one participant who traveled with her brother, or another whose parents approved of her traveling independently. However, some women travel autonomously in spite of these constraints. Unmarried adult women, even those who live away from the family home, may use deception or selective omission in order to avoid opposition from parents to their travel practices. In that vein, I met a number of women who had passed their 20s unmarried (or divorced) and become professionals living on their own. They traveled in Morocco with their cohort of friends, despite having to negotiate gendered obligations to do so, and often without their parents' knowledge.

Creating autonomy

Fedwa is one such woman, describing in Conversation 3.10 her 'normal day' that reaches much further distances than the women previously quoted:

Conversation 3.10 Typical day III

		Fedwa and Mimount, Al Hoceima (Café Miramar), 21 July 2008, 1min
1	LW	what is sort=of a **normal day** (.4) when you come to Morocco/ what=do=you do: (.5) on a normal day
2	M	*<echt allemaal van jou, stel dat die van mij>*
		really all from you, imagine what from me
3	F	[[ahahahahhahahah
4	LW	[[hhhhahahah is there a normal day?
5	F	there is no hh=normal=hh day. .hh bu- normal day, you stay up ((*opstaan*, wake up)), yo- you:: you go:: to have breakfast with your own family, and then/ the **guys** go out**side**, and the **women** stay=at **home** (.) do the **things,** (.3) and you hoping you have a: little bit of time to go to the beach, (.5) we don't go to the beach here because there is all the **family,** so we go to a- a beach, what is eh (.) *beetje* ((*a little*)) feer- eh far, from eh: (.) from here

6	LW	which- eh which beach do you go yo?
7	F	uhm I don't know the names/ I don't know Hoceima: that well that I know the names. (.) but (1.3) I dunno/ we go for like one hour, two hours, come home/ (.9).h have coffee, and/ (.7) come here
8	LW	and- that's- about the same for you ((to M))? yeah.
9	F	yeah that's about the same, the only- difference is, when we go outside Al Hoceima, because we decide always to sta:y like a week, with family/ so we can do everything like/ the **rules**, (.4) of the fami[ly, (.) and then after that week, we go to like eh: (1.4) **Tangier** or eh: **Agadir** or you know/ the big places where you are eh:: (.6) eh:: free to do what you want to do.
10	LW	[yeah/ yeah/
11	LW	well- Agadir is quite far, it must be-#
12	F	yeh it's far/ but hheh if you want to have a nice time [you have to go far=ahahahaha
13	LW	[hheh hehhehheh **really** far. ok: ahhehheh

Fedwa's normal day in Al Hoceima echoes both male and female days described in the previous conversations (3.9 and 3.10) as divided along gender lines. The men go out and the women stay at home, hoping to go out (5). She doesn't manage to spend all day out, but does get out at night; we spoke that evening at Café Miramar (Figure 3.11), a popular, centrally located, and family-friendly café in Al Hoceima.

Figure 3.11 Women-friendly, but still predominantly male, Café Miramar in Al Hoceima. 3 August 2007, 8:30 pm.

Unlike the previously cited women, however, she limits the time she follows the "rules of the family" (9) so that she can go elsewhere. Fedwa solves her problem of limited autonomy by traveling to Agadir, as far as possible from her family home that she can be while still in Morocco. As she laughingly says, "[I]f you want to have a nice time you have to go far" (12). Elsewhere in her interview, she contrasted the 'rules of the family' with her 'normal life' that she regains by traveling elsewhere in Morocco, like her brothers.

> yeah, the- they- they take the car and they go. [(.7) like for a week, (1.2) They don't have to ask/ can we go for a week? no. we are going.

She continued,

> and that is what we want to do too, and you can do that only: if you are an adult and you can say to your parents, ok/# we are going now

Fedwa's assertive attitude, along with other women I met who had similarly negotiated their autonomy to travel, demonstrates how gender prescriptions can be challenged. This conversation actually took place along with Amina, who was reluctant to travel with me to Marrakech, but still had accompanied me out to the café on that evening. While Fedwa draws a sharp contrast between what men and women were permitted to do – which was largely substantiated by male and female participants' activities and tales about their experiences – most women, like Fedwa, seemed to find paths for leisure pursuits that would push and bend the standards that had previously restricted them. Even this café might have been 'off-limits' previously, but had slowly become more populated with groups of autonomous women. Furthermore, as these women become mothers, they may translate their experiences into different allowances and restrictions for the next generations ("Attachments: Perpetuating the Habit in the Next Generation").

Family and autonomy

While these narratives of daily activities and (sometimes unmet) desires for leisure consumption are not explicitly linked to seeing family, they do imply a relationship between staying at 'home' with family and limitations on autonomous practices of mobility. In order to have fun, both male and female DVs want to go out, but generally not to the point of excluding family visits entirely. For most participants, visiting family enters into their idea of being on holiday in Morocco and is part of their typical day. Yet by creating autonomy of mobility to pursue their own leisure, they also limit contact with those family members who are not able to accompany them, for whatever reason. Family visits are thus limited to convenient times and spaces, when DVs choose to make them, to the extent that they can make that choice. The ability to make this choice is intensely tied to both geographies of leisure consumption, in the accessibility of leisure sites nearby, but more embedded in geographies of gendered mobility in Morocco. More than any other dimension, gendered access to autonomous mobility delineates who can leave the diasporic house, and how far he or she can go.

x Attachments: Perpetuating the habit in the next generation

As the migrating generation gives way to their children, and their children's children, the intensity of family connection between branches in Morocco and in Europe can shift. Although visiting specific Moroccan-based family members may no longer be a significant motivator to travel to Morocco, the sense of family connectedness can continue with different motivations. As previous vignettes show, 'family' alone is not the driving factor for return ("Insulations: Familial Obligations"; "Insulations: A Typical Day") but family members and the chance for family gatherings can still play a part in encouraging DV vacation in Morocco.

A number of participants remarked that the visit is important for their children, as a way of showing children "where they come from," or their "point de repères" (point of reference). This desire, however, was tempered with the intention of making the visits more enjoyable – ridding them of the difficulties of arduous travel, unwanted family obligation, or dissatisfactions with the holiday that participants had experienced in their own youth. Many participants made a distinction between their own experiences as children, often infused with monotony and restricted to the diasporic home ("Embodiments: Gendered Boredom"), and the way they want their own children to experience Morocco.

My conversation with Ahlame and Soumia provides one example of how some participants talked about perpetuating the habit of visiting. This topic was particularly relevant to Ahlame, who was pregnant at the time that we spoke, but not as relevant to Soumia, who was in her late 30s and single. Their responses speak to their intentions for their future imminent or possible children, as well as to their lasting impressions of their own holiday experiences (Conversation 3.11):

Conversation 3.11 Bringing children back

Soumia and Ahlame, Antwerp, 25 March 2008, 1min		
1	LW	do you: (1.0) hope that your children will have similar experiences in Morocco as you did? or:: (.) do you plan to bring them back?
		(.7)
2	S	S: oh I never eh t- thought about it, i[t eh ffhhhh/
3	A	[n::e/
		(.8)
4	A	a- it- I think it's important for th- for the children to- to learn the **lang**uage, (1.4) seeing that- the fact that I have a lot of family **there**
5	LW	yeah

6	A	I would like to take my children there. not **ev:ery year** (.9) like we used to go, (.) but u:m: (.6) at least you **go** and meet the **fam**ily and talk to the **fam**ily and **kno:w** (.6) the **fam**ily, (.4) I think that- I- I would think that's important for **my** children, but/ (.5) to spend the same holiday as I spent (.4) ppp (.) I don't know/
7	LW	or t- or even to **see** Morocco:
8	A	to see Morocco, yes. (.6) to s[ee Morocco and to know the family.
9	S	[the- it's impo- (.8) it's important that they know their roots/ eh?=
10	A	y[a
11	LW	[mm
12	S	=from where they are **com**ing and that they speak some **Arab**ic, and so=I don't want (.6 .h) my children: (.4) can speak only Dutch or so/ he,

Ahlame had said previously during this conversation that her family was the most important reason for her to visit Morocco, so it isn't surprising that the experience she imagines for her children is construed through contact with family. However, her proposed visit is not the same annual holiday of her parents – as she emphasized, not every year, but at least to meet the family. Soumia frames her priorities to visit through knowing Arabic, with a preference that her children will not only speak Dutch. Both of these responses reflect aspects of *descent* that are linked to *places* in Morocco – places inhabited either by family or by linguistic roots. Yet they are both adapted for these women's lifestyles: they will not go every year, but enough to be connected in some way.

Putting these intentions into practice can require different kinds of challenges and negotiations. Rabia and Ali are one example of how post-migrant generation parents can perpetuate the habit of visiting (Conversation 3.12). I met them while they were on holiday in Marrakech with one of their small children while the other one was staying with grandparents in France. As parents themselves, Rabia and Ali had already developed a practice of return, which Rabia felt would continue:

Conversation 3.12 Always coming back

Rabia, Marrakech, 13 June 2008, 40sec		
1	LW	par rapport à:: tes enfants, (1.0) tu- (.4) bah j'imagine que::/ (2.0) vous/ continuez à:: (.7) à visiter Maroc eh/ (.9) pendant les années, (.3) tu imagines jamais que: (1.7 .h) un jour vous- vous cessez de (.8) [de venir
		with respect to:: your children, (1.0) you- (.4) well I guess that::/ (2.0) you (pl) are continuing to:: (.7) to visit Morocco eh/ (.9) over the years, (.3) (do) you ever think tha:t (1.7 .h) one day you- you will stop from (.8) [from coming

2	R	[de revenir? ça m'étonnerais, hein (.8) pourquoi non! je pense pas! (.5) peut-être quand on voudra visiter d'autres pays, mais je pense quand-même on va toujours \<passer\> ici/ au pays d'origine
		[from coming back? it would surprise me, yeah (.8) why not! I don't think so! (.5) maybe when we want to visit other countries, but I think anyways we will always \<pass\> here/ in the ancestral country

For Rabia, even if other plans might come up, Morocco was 'obligatory'; it was a "point de repères," she continued, for her children. Like Mounir ("Insulations: Familial Obligations"; "Attachments: Resisting Pressure"), Rabia felt the visit to be obligatory, but accomplished that by maintaining separations between time spent on holiday with her nuclear family in Marrakech and time spent with her parents or her husband's family elsewhere. When I spoke to them, she and her husband were on their leisure holiday in Marrakech, while planning a visit to her in-laws during Ramadan.

For Soumia, Ahlame, and Rabia, visiting Morocco has a positive, fundamental, and formative influence, inferring that children will benefit from 'knowing their roots' through first-person exposure. Yet the idea of return is limited to temporary stays and conscribed by other interests and commitments, and other "point de repères." Rabia's husband Ali expressed how visiting Morocco too long could become 'heavy' (Conversation 3.13):

Conversation 3.13 Not staying too long

Ali, Marrakech, 13 June 2008, 1min		
1	LW	mais- maintenant ça change un peu comme eh:: (.4) là vous pass- vous passez une semaine (.4) à peu près, eh:/ ici à Marrakech, et puis:
		but now it's changing a little like eh:: (.4) no you spen- you are spending a week (.4) just about, eh:/ here in Marrakech, and then:
2	A	ouais, ouais une semaine, à Marrakech, euh:: une semaine, euh:: à Essaouira, fin/ pour voir la famille, (1.0) et euh::: mais j'en ai- fin **nous**, nous depuis qu'on:: est marié, on essaie que faire les deux semaines, pas plus [hein/ (.) parce=que après, moi je crois que c'est un peu:: (.6) lourd
		yeah, yeah one week, in Marrakech, uh:: one week, uh:: in Essaouira, well/ to see the family, (1.0) and uh::: but I've- well **we**, we since we've been married, we try to do the two weeks, no more [yeah/ (.) cause after, me I think that it's a bit:: (.6) heavy
3	LW	[ouais
		[yeah
4	LW	comment ça?
		how's that?
5	A	trop long
		too long
6	LW	ah oui/
		ah yes/

7	A	trop long. qu[and on reste trop long au Maroc, c'est an:: c'est après ça fa- à un moment ça/ (.8) ça va bien, ça suffit,
		too long. wh[en we stay too long in Morocco, it's an:: it's after that it- at a point it/ (.8) it's fine, it's enough,
8	LW	[et bah-
		[oh well
9	LW	donc vo[us-
		so yo[u-
10	A	[plus=que=trois semaines, ça serai trop long pour moi.
		[more=than=three weeks, it would be too long for me.
11	LW	ah oui,
		oh yes,
12	A	moi je peux pas rester, eh::::: (1.5) comme ça, tan/ un mois, un mois et démi, eh::/ (.7) même vivre au Maroc, moi je pourrai pas=hein,
		me I can't stay, eh::::: (1.5) like that, so/ one month, a month and a half, eh::/ (.7) even live in Morocco, me I couldn't=yeah
13	LW	Mmm
		(1.3)
14	A	pour passer les vacances, c'est bon, mais pas pour vivre,=bah=je=ne=sais pas, moi je suis bien chez moi ehhhehehehee
		for spending holidays, it's good, but not for living,=well=I=don't=know, me I'm good at my house ehhhehehehee
((child interruption, 8.1 sec excised))		
15	A	donc il:::: faut:: (.) faudra grandir ici, hein:: (.7) on n'a pas nos points de repare::- nos points de repères, ils sont là où on est né,
		so you:::: must:: (.) got to grow up here, yeah:: (.7) we don't have our points of refare::- our points of reference, they're there where we were born,

While Ali is amenable to visiting Morocco – both on vacation in Marrakech and to his family in Essaouira – he feels the need to limit these visits in length. Similarly to Ahlame, he does not imagine his future visits following his parent's example, spending up to six weeks there on holiday. Furthermore, he cannot imagine living there; in fact, in contrast to his wife, he situates his "points de repères" in France where he was born, not in Morocco.

The combined responses from Ahlame, Soumia, Rabia, and Ali show some of the multifaceted ways that the holiday is practiced, and may continue to be practiced by future generations. These DV parents and potential parents intend to create a vacation in Morocco that they enjoy, and that their children might enjoy, so that they can maintain a connection to different aspects of *descent* that remain there in *place*. These range from encouraging linguistic aptitude in Arabic (Soumia) to ensuring that the younger generation has memories of family households in Morocco (Ahlame). Yet the trajectory of *descent* is not always straightforward: they gather around ideas of rootedness in Moroccan *places*, but not necessarily in the same manner or to the same extent. Rabia is firm in the importance of visiting Morocco for her children, as a way to connect them to her *repères*, while her husband considers his *points de repères* to be in France. These do not necessarily contradict each other: as their children have their own experiences of France and Morocco, their sense of attachment will undoubtedly develop in ways that take on the influences of their parents and peers in how they center their points of reference ("Insulations: Flirting").

xi Insulations: Mentality and distrust

Across the diverse spectrum of DV participants, 'mentality' was a term that came up again and again in interviews as a description for a specific 'Moroccan' way of thinking that is markedly different from their own. In each case, it referred to a sense of distrust – whether of individuals, institutions, or representatives of government institutions. By identifying a negative, opposing behavior, 'mentality' becomes an insulating boundary against which DVs differentiated themselves from Morocco and resident Moroccans.

'Mentality' was sometimes used in a very generic way – not necessarily identifying a specific behavior but a general attitude. Jamila B used it (The Hague, 12 April 2008), for example, in response to a question I asked her about being able to go out by herself when she was growing up. In her answer, she contrasts her behavior in Belgium versus in Morocco:

> yeah! yeah, (.8) to the: **city**::, go to **work**, go to **school**, alone/ (.8) yes/I mean::e:- (1.8) *je **kent** het land, ook eh/ je bent geboren dar, dus/*((you **know** the place, also eh/ you were born there, so/)) eh: yo- eh- you know everythi::ng eh there. (.5) and in Morocco you **don't**, (1.0 .h) they have eh: another mentality [eh: too, (.6) e:::m: (.) eh:: you **can't** eh:m/ (.9) it's- it's a little bit hard to say it but you can't **trust** them/ =

Jamila's distrust encompasses various dangers of Moroccan 'mentality' that emerge in a general public space. She does not apply it to specific actors, using it instead to differentiate her feeling of familiarity with public space in Belgium and unfamiliarity or uncertainty in Morocco.

Similar disconnections in 'mentality' were testified to by others but applied more specifically to actors, like border agents demanding a Moroccan identity card and creating tension about belonging ("Embodiments: Crossing Borders"). Beyond the border agents, recurring extortion of DV drivers by local Moroccan police was also a common complaint that showed a 'mentality' difference in Morocco. In Conversation 3.14 at a café in Al Hoceima, the language shifted from English to Dutch as Fedwa told Mimount, Amina C, and me a story about her brother, here called T--, being stopped by the police and pressured for a bribe:

Conversation 3.14 They won't come back

		Mimount, Fedwa and Amina C, Al Hoceima, 22 July 2008, 1m10s
1	M	wat voor moeilijkheden hebben jullie meegemaakt dan onderweg/ een keer/
		what kind of difficulties did you meet then on the road/ once/
2	F	moeilijkheden? (4.2) nee, over die politieagenten/ die zomaar gewoon mense:::n aanhouden en gewoon, ((deep voice)) je **licht** doet het niet. (.4) T-- zei **#** 1- e- m'n licht doet het nu wel, heb je nog wat?=
		difficulties? (4.2) no, about those police officers/ that just takes aside peo:::ple and like, ((deep voice)) your **light** is not working. (.4) T-- said **#** my light is working now, is there something else?=
3	M	Jea
		Yeah
4	F	=pa**pier**en, waar is je **rijbewijs**, waar is dit, waar is dat, dus zegt ie op <een=gegeven=moment> hier heb je [ook nog de **douane**papieren ja, daar wordt je gewoon misselijk van/ toch?
		=**pa**pers, where is your **driving license**, where is this, where is that, so <at one point> he said here are [my **customs** papers also yeah, it just makes you nauseous/ right?
5	M	[oh::/:::::,
6	A	ja, als het elke keer gebeurt
		yeah, if it happens every time
7	F	ja!
		yes!
8	A	ja. (.7) maar dat do[en ze elke=keer bij de jongens,[(.) mannen/ en zo, vooral jon- jonge jongens, (.4) ze willen gewoon geld, (.7) meestal/ ik ga 't maar niet te hard!
		yes. (.7) but they do[that every=time with the boys, [(.) men/ and so, especially youn- young boys, (.4) they just want money, (.7) mostly/ I better not ((talk)) too loud!
9	LW	[*this is your brother?*
10	F	[*yeah*
		((F and M laughing .6))
11	M	nou, dat is gewoon zo,
		well, thats just the way it is,
12	F	nee nee/ maar: i-i-ik vind 't gewoon een beetje lullig, dan komen ze hier hun vakantie **doorbreng**[en dan=worden ze iedere keer om de haverklap **aan**gehouden/ dat ik denk van ja, zo:/ krijg je ze niet vaker binnen/ je moet[ze echt anders gaan aanpakken ehheeeeheehe
		no no/ bu:t I-I-I find it just a little **stu**pid, they then come here to spend their vacati[on then=every=time, every time like clockwork they are taken as**ide**/ which makes me think yeah, so:/ this is how you won't get them in more often/ you will[really have to treat them differently ehheeeeheehe

In Fedwa's story, the police first cite a non-working tail light as the reason for the stop, which her brother knows to be working. Then, the police continue to demand papers – she lists his driving license and other unnamed documents. In response, she describes that her brother offered the customs paper as well – the form that imported cars are required to carry to prove their tax status as visitors in Morocco. This act on his part underscores that the source of his being stopped is foreign status and not any actual malfunction of the car. Fedwa finally comments that the whole thing nauseates her.

Amina's response to Fedwa's story shows how it resonates as familiar among DVs. Her insertions during and comments after Fedwa tells the story indicate that she understands Fedwa's unspoken implication: that the police were looking for a bribe, particularly from a young man (6). Her sense of distrust extends into the context of the conversation – speaking Dutch in a very popular café in the center of town, she censors herself for criticizing 'too loud' (8).

Fedwa predicts that this kind of behavior will deter people like her brother from spending their vacation in Morocco. Indeed, other DVs talked about similar 'mentality' differences that made them feel not at home in Morocco. In response to a question about whether or not they felt welcome while in Morocco, both Otman and Naim framed their answers in relation to perceived economic differences between themselves and resident Moroccans. In this extract (Conversation 3.15), Naim shifted his response from an economic position in relation to the general population to discuss sources of distrust and harassment by government representatives:

Conversation 3.15 It's not my country

Naim B and Otman B, Antwerp, 25 March 2008, 1m15s		
1	N	I have **really** the feeling that they don't like us. the- they **really** don't like us. (.8 .h) they just li- they just like our **money**, (.4) and then we have to go/ (.) that's it. (.6) just when you- ((swallowing 1.3)) y=know I- I have **two** stress moments in Morocco. one wh- when we arrive in Morocco, (.) for you=know [from: the bo- yeah the customs, (.4) and then when we go back.
2	LW	[the:/ customs, yeah (.) yeah I know about th-
3	LW	cause the-/ I know:: I- I've heard stories about like/ they hassle you: particularly, (.5) to ha- **see**: your::/ carte nationale, from Morocco, and things like that/
4	N	yea::h, ok: that's no problem/ but- but (.6) eh::m (.) then they sa:y like ok/ they have a lot of stuff in your **car**, and you say:::/ y=know/ and then they say ya **op**en **everything** or give me some money. [they really- (.4) the corrup[tion is everywhere. and- and- (.6) and also, (.5) not like that- also, if we<'re> just on the **streets**, and- and-/ the **police** (.7) eh pull us **over** and say yeah/ we're driving **t:oo much**, (.7) ah no [**too fast** and even- and that's **not true** but he just say then he say like ok/ just gimme some coffee[. something to drink a coffee, and then/ (.5) # ya an- these are- those are th- the moments that we **reall:y ha:te** Morocco/ (1.1) **reall:y ha:te** you know like/ in my heart, I=say=like/ this country is not my country. ffft.

He describes similar police behaviors to those Fedwa and Amina described in Conversation 3.14. Naim relates his reaction to these behaviors – being extorted at the border or by the police – as a profound feeling of disconnection from Morocco.

The current of distrust runs counter to positive senses of *attachment*, which envision an unproblematic insertion of DVs into Morocco during the summer ("Attachments: Habitual Mobilities"). Perceptions of pervasive untrustworthy behavior insulate DVs from feeling comfortable with many agents of Moroccan authorities or sometimes even resident Moroccans in general public space. It is no coincidence that the encounters prompting distrust tend to occur in contexts where DVs are easily identifiable – crossing the border with foreign passports, or in cars marked with European license plates. Jamila's general sense of distrust, however, demonstrates that the negative associations with 'mentality' are not limited to institutional encounters, but can be felt as part of general, broad uncertainty about how things are 'different' in Morocco.

xii Embodiments: Gendered boredom

Sometimes *insha'allah* becomes inverted. For many DVs, at certain moments during the holiday, they find themselves becoming bored. Like Anderson (2004) describes, their boredom emerges through time-stilling and space-slowing, when their everyday activities become too habituated and constrained, pushing them to seek new diversions. This stilling and slowing happens across many years of visits to Morocco, in the gradual shift from being constrained by parental authority; to exploring their autonomy and mobility across Morocco as youth and young adults ("Insulations: A Typical Day"; "Embodiments: Having a Car"); to sometimes engineering more entertaining and less constraining vacations for their own children ("Attachments: Perpetuating the Habit in the Next Generation"). In all configurations, boredom – whether one's own embodiment of it or one's children – becomes a site to avoid.

For many participants, this experience started with memories of how their childhood vacation became stilled space. They described bucolic childhood experiences in visiting their parents' hometowns, like playing with their cousins, visiting family, making friends, and embodying rural practices in the areas where their diasporic homes are often located, like picking fruit or fetching water from a well ("Attachments: The Nostalgia of 'Home'"). Often, these narratives gave way to a sense of confinement and frustration upon reaching maturity, manifest in desires to see other places in Morocco, get away from the hometown, and participate in more exciting activities. Boredom emerges in this absence of newness, as DVs become attached in circuits of familiar practices and obligated to stay in one place – often at home – and not escape to discover something or somewhere else.

This lack of mobility is often linked either to being confined geographically to an isolated, land-locked Moroccan hometown that lacked in leisure facilities, or being limited in one's autonomy of movement as a woman, or a combination of the two ("Insulations: A Typical Day"). Both men and women might experience boredom, with different individuals developing strategies to access leisure, to be mobile, and to escape. However, limits on women's mobilities generally reflect gendered geographies of women's duties and responsibilities inside the home. In the group interview with Family A, including two brothers (Hassan and Larbi), their sister Yasmine and sister-in-law Lena, I asked about their activities in their small Saharan Moroccan hometown. Immediately preceding this moment, the men in this group had discussed how they sought leisure in their town by borrowing their father's car while he napped to drive out to a nearby natural spring. When I posed the question about different activities for boys or girls, the two men began answering for themselves and also for the women:

Conversation 3.16 Activities for boys and girls

		Hassan, Larbi, Lena, & Yasmine (all A), Roubaix, 1 Feb 2008, 25s
1	LW	il y avait des- de::s activités differents parmi le::s (.5) les gosses et les/
		there were some- some:: different activities between the kids and the/
		(.4)
2	H	les garçons et les fill[es?
		the boys and the gir[ls
3	LW	[ouais=hh les garçons et les filles/
		[yeah=hh the boys and the girls
4	LA	ah oui non c'était pas:::/ les garçons c'est- c'est vrai que t'as la piscine eh:
		ah yes no it was no:::t/ the boys it's- it's true that you have the pool eh:
5	H	ouais nous pouvons aller à la piscine ou [euh:=
		yeah we could got to the pool or [euh:=
6	LA	[ouais
		[yeah
7	H	=ou là on pouvait se balader, on xx entre nous, quoi
		=or there we could walk around, on xx between us, you=know
8	LW	Mm
9	H	les filles, bon/ c'était pa::::::s
		the girls, well/ it wasn::::::'t
10	LA	les filles c'était euh::: bah elles avaient pas beaucoup d'activités en fait! hhh hhh hh
		the girls it was uh::: well they didn't have many activities in fact! hhh hhh hh
11	LE	ça commence, ça commence/ [avoir des activ[ités. **nous** no-notre activité, c'était faire la cui**sine**, eh/ [(.) le ména**ge**-
		it starts, it starts/ [have many activ[ities. **us** ou- our activity, it was doing the **cook**ing, eh/ [(.) the **clean**ing-
12	H	[mais non mais c'est vrai, eh/
		[but no but it's true, eh/
13	LA	[à l'époque
		[at the time
14	Y	Aheheheh

When Larbi and Hassan were at a loss to think of what there was for girls to do, Lena interjected to contradict Hassan's statement that girls didn't have many activities (10): their activities were housework (11).

Yet, this embodiment of 'boredom' is not completely gender divided. Going 'home' to a place like this small town eventually becomes boring both for men and women. It adheres to the first condition noted earlier, being a small, land-locked place, with few leisure sites to keep the month-long family visit exciting. Women, however, may be further constrained by their home-based responsibilities, leaving less opportunity for spontaneous activities outside the house. Men can access more publicly situated forms of leisure consumption in small towns than women can, inasmuch as many of these sites, like local public pools or ordinary cafés, are predominantly sites of male consumption throughout the year. Yet, girls and women are actually more 'active': they are engaged with their 'activities' around the house, while boys and men who are 'on holiday' might in fact have more difficulty finding 'something to do' in the limited leisurescape of a small town.

Whether or not they were permitted – or had the necessary transport ("Embodiments: Having a Car") – to roam in their hometowns, once men reach maturity and have their own capital and access to mobility resources, they tend to escape boredom by traveling independently. Women often continue to be constrained in their mobility by their connections to related men, but many, like Fedwa ("Insulations: A Typical Day"), actively pursue autonomous mobility in defiance of those rules. Others take advantage by joining their brothers' and male cousins' mobilities to pursue their own projects of travel.

For many women, autonomous mobility beyond parental control – or the ability to escape the boredom of the household – arrives with marriage. By entering into a familial relationship in a different role, effectively becoming decision-makers for their own families about how to divide their holiday time between leisure and obligation, married women are no longer constrained in their autonomy, though they still might be constrained by responsibilities of care. Boredom can still then be a factor in choosing leisure activities – but countered by choosing *insha'allah* escapes for the whole family, to keep the children entertained, as well as for one's own leisure pursuits ("Attachments: Touring Elsewhere").

xiii Insulations: Viscous places of protection

Fieldnote extract 3.11 Boys are too aggressive, 29 July 2008

out last night at Arena Palace in Fes, a café set back off of Hassan II, in a neighborhood of banks, nice hotels and govt buildings (plus other nice shops)

I was trying to be determined (not to work) and enjoy some coffee while finishing my cigarettes with A---, but [DVs] just kept coming in. soon, I had my eyes drawn to 3–4 tables at once, trying to decide the best way to approach.

...

talked as well to a table of NL girls, related as sisters/cousins, with family home in fes but other family in other not-close cities – guercif? somewhere near oujda

Nasrine with a sense of humor (or a case of the giggles) whose father wouldn't let them out of the car in Nador because the boys are too aggressive.

her best moment, which wasn't recorded, talking about wanting to be in Tanger (*tan-ger) where there are other hollanders, as opposed to fes where the boys are bad. (1st time I've heard this expressed desire to stay with our own kind, because they are respectful in a way we are used to).

Although I went to this café in order to relax with a friend, the evening turned into another episode of fieldwork. I was unable to resist the lure of making contact with some of the many groups of DVs dotting the tables of Arena Palace. The previously quoted fieldnotes discuss one of the tables I spoke with that night – a group of young Dutch women.

Figure 3.12 Arena Palace café. Fes. 29 July 2008, 10:20 pm.

Our conversation indicated one reason that café was so popular with DVs. As Nasrine told me after I had stopped recording, she would rather be in Tangier (pronounced with Dutch phoneticization, as /tañger/, distinct from the Arabic /tenja/) because that's where other Dutch people are, who are 'respectful' and interact with them in a way that is familiar. Her description alluded to the trope of male 'protection' surrounding Muslim women, whether in Morocco or elsewhere (Freeman 2005). Like many other women in this project – Fedwa, for example, who went on vacation around Morocco ("Insulations: A Typical Day") – had found ways to manage that unwanted attention in order to achieve the autonomous mobility they desired. Quite often, this management involved creating and accessing spaces of permissible mobilities, places their parents considered acceptable and 'protective.' Similarly, this café created a 'protective,' insulating environment, where Nasrine can go out and not be harassed by aggressive boys.

In the absence of an individual male protector, insular geographies of DV leisure act as an encompassing gaze of a known community, deterring unwanted male gazes. Many women found it in their best interest to stay with their 'protector' – whether an individual or a particular setting, like this café – as a strategy for lessening the harassment they might otherwise receive. Women's choices of where to go out – as much as who to go out with – reflect an awareness of and participation in this dynamic. These choices include, for example, going to certain pools or beaches, or going to 'family' cafés, as opposed to the ones populated mostly by men.

Noura, whom I also spoke to at that café that night, expressed this rationale more directly (Conversation 3.17):

Conversation 3.17 Among ourselves

Noura, Fes (Arena Palace Café), 29 July 2008, 30sec		
1	LW	tu m'as dit- que- eh:: tu as dit que:::m (.6) la piscine Zalagh c'est pas- comme c'est tranquille (1.0) tu as eu des::: (.5) j'ai pas. des his**toires**, des expé**ri**ences, (.) euh:: (.3) pas tranquilles? disons?
		you told me- that- eh:: you said that:::m (.6) the Zalagh pool is not- like it's peaceful (1.0) have you had any::: (.5) I dunno. any **stories**, any exp**er**iences. (.) uh:: (.3) not peaceful? let's say?
2	N	eh: oui, parce=que en fait, pour moi je dis Zalagh c'est tranquille,
		eh: yes, because in fact, for me I say Zalagh is peaceful,
3	LW	ouais
		yeah
4	N	parce=qu'il=y=a d'autres piscines, il y a des complexes (.) il=y=a **Trois Sources**, il=y=a **Camping**, il=y=a le (.) le Diamant Vert/ (.9) mais en fait, (.6) euh::m nous, on aime pas se mélanger avec les gens d'ici parce=que les gens d'ici, (.) ehm::: ils aiment ehm: comment- comment dire ça. (1.6) ils aiment euh: (.) nous a**bord**er, et=ils=savent **pas** comment nous aborder. (.3) ils nous abordent eh: (.5) **assez** sauvagement,

		because=there=are other pools, there are complexes (.) there's **Trois Sources**, there's **Camping**, there's the (.) le Diamant Vert/ (.9) but in fact, (.6) uh::m us, we don't like mixing with people from here cause people from here, (.) ehm::: they like to ehm: how- how to say it. (1.6) they like to euh: (.) ap**proach** us, and=they=**don't** know how to approach us. (.3) they approach us eh: (.5) **too** aggressively,
5	LW	ouais
		yeah
6	N	et ils manquent souvent de respect. (.4) et c'est pour ça nous on es**saie**/ surtout les filles, bon les garçons moins parce=que toutes les filles, on essaie de s'éloigner de ces lieux, (.6) et de nous euh/ de nous mettre **entre nous**, (.) entre:: entre immigrés en fait.
		and they are often lacking respect. (.4) and that's why we try/ more so the girls, well the boys less cause all the girls, we try to distance ourselves from those places, (.6) and to keep euh/ to keep ourselves among **ourselves**, (.) among:: among immigrants in fact.
7	LW	ouais
		yeah
8	N	au moins, on se **comprend**, et euh même s'il y a un immigré qui vient côtoyer une fille, (.5) il::- il va pas nous manquer de respect. ou rarement.
		at least, we **understand** each other, and uh even if there's an immigrant who comes next to a girl, (.5) he::- he will not be lacking respect. or rarely.

While Arena Palace was our first interaction, earlier that day I had seen Noura when I went to the Hotel Zalagh pool with Mounir and his friends ("Embodiments: Suntanning"). Noura mentions some of the local swimming pools in Fes – Trois Sources, Camping, Diamant Vert – that are not connected to hotels and cost less to enter. As she describes, keeping away from certain places – like those pools – avoids "lack of respect" exhibited by resident Moroccans. By choosing the Zalagh pool or Arena Palace café, with its evident popularity with DVs, she makes herself less visible to the kind of person with whom she does not want to interact, the resident Moroccan man who is disrespectful; she manages to "keep ourselves among ourselves."

Inasmuch as these leisure geographies involve consumption of spaces where women might choose to be uncovered – beaches, pools, nightclubs – the financial capital insulating these exclusive places becomes an important element to ensure women's comfort and safety there. As Noura explained to me about her attire while sitting in Arena Palace, "During the day, I can't go out in a dress like this." Her clothing that night would not be considered inappropriate in a European café but may be found too revealing out in public in Morocco. The implication, then, is that the café was somehow private. As seen in the image showing Arena Palace (Figure 3.12), clientele sitting in it were somewhat obscured from the street perspective by plants. Beyond the physical environment, however, the café becomes an insulated space populated by like-minded patrons – also DVs – where she can dress how she pleases. Her embodiment as a DV extends beyond her clothing choice to the places she chooses to frequent, which offer her protection from some gazes and access to others. The insulation of viscosity enables her to go out dressed like that, to a place where she can be protected from harassment, even without a male 'protector.'

The presence of the many DV women I found at this café illustrates both Noura's desire for insulated interaction and the *viscosity* of DV leisure practices. By 'sticking together,' Noura and Nasrine help to create protective environments where they can hang out, which move from place to place around Morocco and appear and disappear as DVs show up and depart. These fluid and mobile formations are not necessarily agentively produced; they are practiced as combinations of instinctive and conscious choices that pull like together with like and make a membrane of surface tension against others. These dynamics reflect the complexity of assemblage in the way that certain sites, like Arena Palace, emerge as nodes attracting DV consumers, only to die out as the swarm migrates to another hive, moving individually but in concert. Arena Palace was only a node, to my knowledge, in the year that I performed this fieldwork; when I returned two years later, the restaurant had been closed, with rumors floating of corruption. Yet, the site itself is not unique – a new place popped up to replace it.

xiv Insulations: Viscous places of consumption

The gendered protective environments in cafés in "Insulations: Viscous Places of Protection" show one side of viscosity – how it generates protective borders to keep unwanted others out. Inversely, viscosity also acts to attract like-minded others together. In summertime Morocco, part of what enables that congealing together is DVs' economic capacities for consumption. The cafés and pools they tend to choose are seen as 'higher quality' versions of parallel spaces elsewhere, not just because of their safety from overaggressive male gazes. The pool at Hotel Zalagh costs 100 dirham to enter – the equivalent of approximately 10 Euro, or more than half of a resident Moroccan daily minimum wage. Likewise, the coffee at Arena Palace costs double what you might find elsewhere. All cities I visited, and even some smaller towns, have parallel leisure sites: the aquatic park, the hotel pool, the section of the beach where it is mostly DV sunbathers; the fancy patisserie, café, or ice cream parlor that is mostly the same DVs after the sun goes down during July and August. All such sites are rendered exclusive through higher prices.

What unites these places is their adherence to contemporary globalized modes of consumption, touristic or otherwise for visitors to Morocco. They offer services that have apparent standards of quality relative to the prices paid, making them 'safe' for consumption by non-locals. DVs usually describe them as 'clean,' 'peaceful,' or 'friendly.' When talking about beaches they prefer, 'the beach' usually refers, upon further questioning, to beaches that are 'cleaner' or 'quieter' than other options. In terms of food, DVs share concerns with other visitors about digestive problems resulting from food handling and cooking, and cite that as a reason to choose certain restaurants over others. Likewise, many appreciate Marjane, a chain superstore that has opened across Morocco in increasing numbers in the past ten years because it offers everything in one place with prices posted. Marjane is, in fact, a subsidiary of the French Carrefour group.

Coming from Europe and orienting to European modes of leisure consumption, DVs understandably seek similar means and manner of consumption on holiday. Their pursuits sometimes intersect with foreign tourists, in the same hotels or seeing the same national landmarks. They also intersect with elite resident Moroccans, by consuming at the same salons, cafés, or nightclubs that those residents inhabit ten months of the year. These spaces become insulated because of their normal clients' access to relatively more expendable income, and then come to be viscously inhabited by DVs through their ability to spend. Even if their expendable income is not considered high in their countries of residence, its value-for-service is increased in the cost-of-living differential between Europe and Morocco.

Conspicuous divisions

The emergence of this viscous consumption links these places to conspicuous consumption (Caletrío 2014), or the ways in which consuming as a leisure activity becomes a way to demonstrate one's access to capital (see "Embodiments: Diasporic, Touristic, Citizens"). It becomes linked to attitudes about status – particularly in raising one's own status through actively demonstrating wealth and thereby lowering the status of others who do not match consumption habits. In this vein, an impression was repeated to me by resident Moroccans that the visitors are actively 'showing off' their wealth in the way they consume. Even some DVs echoed this impression, as with Soumia in Conversation 3.18, talking about the kind of people she encountered hanging out on the beach in Morocco:

Conversation 3.18 The way they're sitting there

Soumia and Ahlame, Antwerp, 25 March 2008, 40sec		
1	LW	if you're out on the beach, or::/ when you're **outside**/ (.) eh: (1.4 .h) who is it that you end up seeing mostly/ is it em:: (.) like- do you see a lot of other kharij, other:: like visitors? or are you seeing Moroccans who live there? Or
2	S	I don't like the beach (.) first, and two/ when i go to the beach, because (.3) you **have** to go to the beach when you are in Moroc[co, I see a lot of people who are living in Europe!
3	LW	[ahhehehe
4	LW	Yeah
		(2.0)
5	S	a **lot** of people.
6	LW	how can you tell? is it ju- language? or
7	S	[[the language, the manner, eh to:/ (.) # (.8) to be **there**, ((stirring tea))(.6) a little bit arrogance too (.4) °I think°
8	A	[[mm (.7) mmmm
9	LW	yeah, mm. (.4) really. arrogance.

10	S	yea:: just eh.) **yes,** arrogance.
11	LW	why? wh–
12	S	um: (1.4) the way they **speak,** the way they- they're **sitting** there, and thinking that eh: (.7) because they have some **money** they: they can do everything. I don't know, it's a (1.4) it's a feeling.

Soumia's impressions about the 'arrogance' of diasporic Moroccans on the beach match an idea of a conspicuous consumer: demonstrating higher status through money and attitudes. As she says, "[B]ecause they have some money…they can do everything." Though Soumia could potentially fit into this exclusive category – she is, of course, a diasporic visitor and someone who also has access to some money to spend during her vacation in Morocco – she recognizes how the attitude of exclusivity can make 'the beach' viscously unwelcoming. She does not want to spend time there, at least in part because it is dominated by 'arrogant' people living in Europe.

For most DVs, I do not believe the decision to spend time in relatively expensive, 'quality-controlled' places comes out of a targeted or conscious desire to avoid resident Moroccans. Many make directed efforts to participate and belong in that community and want to feel accepted as part of the 'local' community (see Wagner 2015). Yet many still hang out in places that are effectively excluding; even Soumia, who is disdainful of how 'arrogant'

Figure 3.13 Playa beach, Al Hoceima. 29 July 2007, 5:30 pm.

attitudes are on display at the beach, might choose a more expensive café when she goes out, without considering how that choice can insulate her as a leisure consumer.

This insulation as consumers may not be wholly intended, yet it serves to reinforce several boundaries that many participants found important to make for their comfort as visitors. For some, like Noura, going to the Hotel Zalagh pool or the Arena Palace café is a result of feeling harassed in other parallel consumption places. For others, that decision might be a desire for quality assurance and embodied comfort – like choosing to stay in a hotel with air conditioning and not in the family home. For others still, such decisions might result through their social networks: in connecting with family, peers, or friends, they experience certain places, and return along with other peers, or move on to the next interesting spot. The effect of this circulation of information, interconnected geographies, and mobilities is *viscosity*, making DVs increasingly insulated from resident Moroccans who are not able to access the same places.

Intensive embedding

The viscosity of DV mobilities became evident to me as I became more embedded in their flows over the course of my fieldwork. Similarly to Saldanha (2007), I began to be able to predict the flows of people from one site to the next, in repeating patterns, which varied day to day but stuck to the same kinds of sites and timespaces. This circulation and repetition came to a point where I became absorbed into the *viscosity* of DV networks myself. I began to coincidentally rediscover participants I had known elsewhere. For example, on the day that I accompanied Mounir to the Hotel Zalagh pool, I noticed a woman chatting by the bar; later that day I found her, Noura, in a café. While I was in Marrakech stopping at a McDonald's with a group of Belgian DVs, I was spotted by one of the Dutch students I had met earlier in the summer. Between our meetings, she had been back to the Netherlands and returned to Morocco for her normal family visit to Rabat. Most surprisingly, in the restroom of a hotel pool in Meknes, a French DV recognized me from a rest stop on the road in Spain, where I had approached friends of hers with survey questionnaires. All of these places of consumption are connected through a viscous geography that crosses the European trajectory into and throughout Morocco, allowing DVs to float along surfaces (Stewart 2007) of consumption spaces in Morocco and congregate in nodes of mutual attraction.

One such node, where DVs were predictably to be found, is McDonald's. Early in the Moroccan phase of fieldwork, I was told by taxi drivers to look for DVs at McDonald's. I followed this advice but found it fruitless early in the summer. Later, after mid-July when the majority of European school vacation begins, the situation reversed. I was brought to McDonald's (Figure 3.14) by three separate DVs in different cities.

Figure 3.14 McDonald's Meknes. 17 August 2008, 10:45 pm.

Like other consumption sites incorporated into this insulated DV web, McDonald's is a source of 'quality' in their terms. The food there is trusted not to cause digestive problems. It is more expensive than a meal in a typical sandwich place, but still cheaper than in Europe. One participant explained part of the reasoning for choosing it over local sandwich places: DVs cannot eat McDonald's in Europe because the meat is not halal. That said, McDonald's is not empty when the DVs are not there: it is equally, I discovered early in the summer, a place for middle-class Moroccans to hang out. Most importantly for the dynamics of DV insulations, McDonald's is accessible by car ("Embodiments: Having a Car").

xv Embodiments: Having a car

> **Fieldnote extract 3.12 Looking for people or cars? 3 August 2008**
>
> earlier when I talked to [resident vendor participant], he said all the hollanders were here last week. also, that I should look in the parking lot behind the hotel CTM or the one by koutoubia to find their cars. why do people always direct me to their cars?

Figure 3.15 Predominantly European license plates, parked at an outlying beach near Al Hoceima. 31 July 2007, 5 pm.

When I chatted with taxi drivers, vendors, and other local residents about where to find DVs, they would often refer me to places their cars were parked. In Fieldnote Extract 3.12, the vendor refers me to parking lots near central landmarks just outside of Djemaa el Fna; places where these cars might be parked during a day trip to the old city. Yet my questions were never posed as "where can I find their cars" but as "where can I find these people." Ethnomethodologically, I have to take their answers as relevant to how DVs are visible in Morocco: through their cars. Sending me to where their cars sit reflects on how intensively DV presence is embodied through their automobility – their access to and use of cars.

Car bodies

Cars as material objects of consumption are densely packed signifiers of economic status, interwoven with potential mobilities and blockages (Merriman 2009; Miller 2001). The way they mark the user's social and economic status can go far beyond their practical use for transport. For example, Truitt (2008) traces motorbikes in Vietnam as a commodity occupying a vibrant intersection of trade liberalization and control over urban mobilities, which consolidates in an assemblage of the emerging Vietnamese middle class. New access to wealth, along with new access to international trade and new reasons for increasing travel distances around the city flow together into making motorbikes a key form of transport. But motorbikes also entail new forms of embodied, material and social entanglement. They make possible close contact between couples while riding them, breaking taboos of intimacy; they reformulate urban traffic to accommodate the critical mass of motorbikes on the road; they render legible the hierarchies of foreign brands as class signifiers; and they surpass bicycles as vehicles, increasing speed, pollution, and a sense of frenetic freedom and flexibility across the landscape.

Many of these same transformations resonate with the cars temporarily imported by DVs and families during the summer months in Morocco. These cars foster potential for illicit intimacy, create blockages in urban traffic flows, are potently identifiable with foreign brands and class signifiers, and become integral to feelings of speed and mobility around Morocco. The major difference is the source of the commodity. Instead of local residents demonstrating upward economic mobility in a critical mass, the economic distinctiveness applies to diasporic families in a brief, intense flood.

Very high tax on importation of used cars, plus the prohibitively high pricing of new cars means that car ownership in Morocco remains an important class distinction (Ksikes et al. 2009). Compared to most European nations, where car ownership is well over 400 per thousand, Morocco was home to 53 cars per thousand persons in 2007 (World Bank n.d.). According to government tabulations of entries of persons and cars by ferry, MNRA temporarily imported about 700,000 cars during the summer of 2008, increasing the population of vehicles in Morocco by nearly 50%. Following these figures, MNRA presence in Morocco is embodied along with their cars.

As much as these cars serve as instruments for experiencing forms of mobility, they are also material objects that reflect significations of wealth and consumption. As described by Faiza Guène in her fictional perspective on a family leaving for Morocco (Chapter 1 – "Introduction"), (over)loading the family car with goods is a visible trope embedded in diasporic travel. Furthermore, cars entering from Europe – easily identifiable by their European license number plates – are recognizable as consumption objects themselves. Brands of cars have become increasingly important as part of conspicuous consumption displayed on the extension of the driver's body. Many participants told me, although none claimed to have done it, about young DVs saving money to rent expensive models to drive for the summer. Yet beyond how cars can signify economic power as cultural objects, they also enable mobility and extend embodiment in the way they move through and take up space. How and where cars go, and how they occupy space in the process, are intensely visible and closely read.

Car distances

For average resident Moroccans, daily mobilities encompass a territorial span that reflects their access to transport. With private automobile ownership being so limited, this often means using public transport, with its costs, unreliabilities, discomforts, and demands for time. Journeys involving the aid of transport, from one side of the city to another, for example, are undertaken for good reason or for a stay of a proportionate duration. Movement

Figure 3.16 Traffic clogging a main road in Al Hoceima. 2 August 2007, 10 pm.

for the sake of movement tends to be practiced on foot, as many city streets are crowded in the evenings with pedestrians going out to stroll. Automobiles might participate in this 'strolling' to some extent, but acting much more as symbols of class distinction, dividing their drivers (with capital) from those who walk (without capital).

Many DVs participate in pedestrian mobilities along with their family members, or as a site for leisure they might enjoy themselves. DVs, however, also usually have access to a car – meaning that they also, perhaps more than resident Moroccan family and peers, can more easily 'stroll' to more distant and exclusive places. They may not realize that they are participating in an exclusive form of leisure mobility, as illustrated in this part of my conversation with Anissa and Shirin (Conversation 3.19). I started by asking them about the characteristics of the beaches they like to go to:

Conversation 3.19 Beaches for people who have a car

Anissa and Shirin, Den Haag, 10 April 2008, 1m30s		
1	LW	what about um: going to **beach**/ I know- (.8) um- some people tell me about- you know/ beaches in Morocco have different kind=if **characteristics** like/ there's the beach where everyone is going to show **off** and there's the bea[ch where it's more **families**, and- (.4) um, what kinds of- (.4) do you go to all different kinds? or are there particular ones that you like/

2	S	[yeah
3	A	I go to/ (.) different ones, [(.) I don't really pay attention t[o: (.4) like, (1.4) **no**, (.) to the people or anything like that/
4	LW	[yeah [no?
5	S	we don't yeah=
6	A	=like if I'm in: El Jadida I go to Sidi Bouzid, (.) that's um: it's- it's not the beach of El Jadida, but it's [(.6) near- nearby,=
7	S	[Sidi Bouzid is a nice/ (.) yeah. nearby:
8	A	=and (.4) you see (.) **all** kinds of people there. (.) a lot of **families**, a lot of **youngsters**,
9	S	but that's a **good** one because for us it's **diff**erent/ my dad, (.9) he let us go to the she- to the beach but h- eh:: (.) not to the beach of **Rabat** because everyone is going to the beach of Rabat, all the (.) e::m (1.0) a lot of **boys**, eh::::: it's **easier** for them, so my dad s- g- always say, go to the beach, but the **beach** where (.) no **bus**es are driving=hhhahahahah so only peopl:::e who have a **car** can go to that beach, [so it's (1.0) normally eh:: yeah **Temara** or **Bouznika** or some eh- somewhere else. (.) cause Rabat is **very full** then [(1.4) a lot of boys,
10	A	[mmmm,
11	LW	[mmm
12	LW	Yeah
13	S	more boys than the girls. so that's why,

Figure 3.17 A car-accessible beach: Achakar, near Tangier. 5 July 2008, 5:45 pm.

Although Anissa begins this discussion by saying she goes to 'different beaches,' seemingly non-exclusively, the beach she cites in line 6, Sidi Bouzid, fits into the dynamic of DV consumption of more exclusive places. Nearly 30 years before this study, Berriane noted that specific beach as frequented by elite resident Moroccans on holiday (1980). Anissa may not realize that it is considered 'exclusive,' in that it may be for her relatively similar to other beaches in the area. Shirin, however, counters her friend's indifference by describing how certain beaches near her diasporic home in Rabat are considered 'better' by her father because of how they are accessed. Her father tells her to go to beaches where the buses do not reach – meaning to relatively inaccessible places that are more difficult to access without a car. Figure 3.17 is one example of a beach like that, where during summer it remains relatively less busy. Many other DVs mentioned 'seclusion' and 'isolation' as characteristic of the beaches they prefer, implying their ability to reach them when others cannot. While Anissa may be practicing exclusive beach leisure consumption without realizing it, Shirin is directed to do so, as a way of avoiding a place that is too 'full.'

The Arena Palace café, the main site of activity in the vignette "Insulations: Viscous Places of Protection," is another example of a location that functions, and becomes a site for leisure, because of its car accessibility. When I was there, it was a solitary energetic site on what was otherwise a boulevard full of banks and government buildings already closed for the evening. It has an ample and accessible car park in front of it, with plenty of room for DV vehicles (Figure 3.18).

Figure 3.18 Cars congregating outside Arena Palace, Fes. The major part of the parking area is behind this perspective, out of frame.

In "Insulations: Viscous Places of Protection," Noura told me about her swimming pool preferences: much like Anissa and Shirin, she named different public swimming pools in Fes – all of which are more accessible by public transport and less expensive than the hotel where I first met her – as places she would rather not go. That night Nasrine also told me how her father would not let her out of the car in Nador ("Insulations: Viscous Places of Protection"). Whether purposeful or not, car-based consumption contributes to the places DVs can access and choose to go as elite consumers in their nodes of viscosity, separating them from a public and collecting them in a group. In connection with controlling their *viscous* environments, the distance and accessibility of these places relate to the economic power of their clientele in a way that DVs are kept 'safe' and seek out others like them.

Car visibility

Only by "following the people" was I able to actually see these sites that might otherwise be invisible. By the end of the summer, I began to realize that most new places I was being taken to by DVs were new to me because I had been unable to find them on my own, without a car. I was led to car-friendly cafés, with ample parking on the surrounding streets or car parks beside them; not the cafés on the central boulevards or in the old city centers which are easy to discover by walking but require parking at a distance. The McDonald's found in most of the larger cities are nearly all equipped with their own parking and some with drive-thru windows as well ("Insulations: Viscous Places of Consumption"). Likewise, aquatic parks and desirable beaches are always away from the center, sometimes difficult to reach by public transport but always difficult to return from by public transport. Once distanced from the center, the non-automobile passenger either must pay the higher prices extorted for independent mobility by paying a taxi to travel out and back, or wait for an empty place in a passing taxi whose driver is willing to stop. Either way requires a frustrating investment of uncertain capital that is nullified by having the appropriate private car.

DV cars are materially cogent to the way the holiday happens. Their movement into Morocco by car is a highly visible, recorded event ("Embodiments: Crossing Borders"), but their movements around Morocco are less easily tracked (but still trackable). They might convene in places, like the center of Marrakech or Tangier, that are publicly visible, but they also congeal around places that are relatively invisible – like the distant beaches and aquatic parks they seek out to find peaceful leisure. These places are effectively invisible to those I was asking in the central, pedestrian city – like the resident vendor participant at the start of this vignette who told me to look in parking lots. These vehicle-accessible places, like the aquatic parks and distant beaches that render DVs materially 'invisible' in cityscapes by removing their cars, are densely populated in the map of *viscous* DV leisure consumption geographies.

xvi Attachments: Touring elsewhere

Anissa and Shirin in Conversation 3.20 recount a common story about their family habits of visiting Morocco. Even as adults, they are enthusiastic about the visit and consistently go with their families ("Attachments: Habitual Mobilities"). Yet they also imagine exploring elsewhere, as do their siblings, and sometimes act on these desires:

Conversation 3.20 Go somewhere else

		Anissa and Shirin, Den Haag, 10 April 2008, 1m30
1	LW	before, this year/ (.4) um (2.0) what was- (.4) the kind of normal cycle with your family/ you went every year:? every other year:,
2	A	al:most every year.
3	S	ya we went **every** year
4	LW	and it's- **everyone** in the family? no exception? or eh
5	S	**ev**eryone. (.4) **ev**eryone is hh=going=hhehehehe
6	A	no xxx
7	S	Yeah
8	A	xx
9	S	<ons> wel but we li- we **want** to go/ so we **like** to go, so that's like, it was not (1,0) *het was niet erg of zo, wij* **wil***den juist gaan/ dus eh:: (1.0) ja* it was not bad or something, in fact we wanted to go/ so eh:: (1.0) yes
		(1.6)
10	LW	[[it's
11	A	[[*nee ja, bij ons was het ook eigenlijk zo dat eh mijn zussen soms ergens anders naar toe wilden* [[no yes, with us it was actually also that my sisters sometimes wanted to go somewhere else
12	S	*Ja* Yes
13	A	*naar een ander land* to some other country
14	S	*ja dat hebben wij bij* **nu** *dan. nu we ouder zijn geworden hebben wij dat weer,* [*dat begrijp ik wel.* yes we have that now. now that we have become older we have that again, [I do understand that.
15	A	*ja, want ik ben ook een keertje niet mee geweest en dat ik naar Portugal ging met vriendinnen en dat zij wel naar* [*Marokko gingen* (.6) *of m'n zus dat* (.6) *ze naar Griekenland ging/ en m'n ouders wel naar Marokko/ dus,* yes, because I once did not go with [them] either because I went to Portugal with friends ((female)) and they did [go to Morocco (.6) or my sister that (.6) she went to Greece/ and my parents still went to Morocco/ so,
16	S	[*ja*
17	S	*ja dat hebben wij bij nu,* (.) *maar eer-, vroeger niet. vroeger gingen we gewoon mee. en toen wilden we ook meegaan/ nou, vroeger, dan heb ik het over vier jaar geleden/ drie jaar geleden/* (.5) *maar sinds toen is het nu eh nu ga ik ook niet meer elk jaar mee en ehm*

		yes, we have that now, (.) but earl-, before no. previously we just went along. and also then we wanted to go/ well, previously, then I'm talking about four years ago/ three years ago/ (.5) but since then it is eh now I don't go along every year anymore and ehm
18	LW	*yeah I know- it seems like that changes arou:nd (.) you know/ eighteen years old/ nineteen years ol[d/ people start to think (.6) like, I don't have to go::/ if I don't want to=hhhehehe*
19	S	[ja ja dan begint het. ja/ (1.5) ja/ (.) ja
		[yes yes that's when it starts. yes/ (1.5) yes/ (.) yes
20	A	*there are more countries than Morocco!*
21	S	[[yeah! there are mo::re! rea:lly/
22		[[((LW and A laughing))

In this conversation (Conversation 3.20), the two women start from the position of wanting to go along with their parents and families, and by the end of the sequence arrive at the agreement that there are "more countries than Morocco!" (20) Though they can still express attachment to Morocco by visiting – I met them when they were visiting together as two young adult women in Marrakech, independently from their families – their desire to go elsewhere expresses how their sense of attachment differs from their parents.

For many participants, this more complicated sense of attachment first manifested in wanting to stop and visit in other cities along the way to Morocco. They complained that their parents were disinterested in seeing any of the beauty of the passing landscape, much less stopping to tour in any of the well-known cities they pass through on the most common route from the Netherlands, Belgium, and northern France – including Paris, Bordeaux, and Madrid. Yet, as Wolbert (2001: 21) observes in looking at photographs taken by Turkish migrants driving from Germany, the duration of the voyage becomes a 'border'; Austria and the former Yugoslavia are unidentifiable images through the windscreen. For the migrating generation, their direct, lived attachment to the destination in Morocco is often the main reason to visit; the intervening landscape is simply something to be crossed. For post-migrant generations, whose familial and emotional attachment to Morocco is differently construed than their parents, the route holds potential attractions as much as, or more than, the destination.

This unwillingness to tour has two primary effects. First, the unseen sites become more desirable to post-migrant passengers who do not have the same goal as their parents. Second, it renders the drive 'boring,' repetitious, and therefore disagreeable for some, as one anticipates that nothing 'exciting' (*insha'allah*) will happen. Cousins Otman and Naim B described how their parents are focused solely on the destination, like a 'one-way ticket' to Morocco. Everything in between was unimportant. Yet, in recent years, their parents have also participated in touring other places – specifically in *places* that resonate to them as sites of Moroccan history, like Granada, Spain.

One such touring visit to Granada happened during my travel with Family B in a caravan of family and extended family on the way to Morocco

("Embodiments: Starting the Journey"). It was a rare example of *insha'allah* serendipity enacted by the migrating generation rather than by their children. The following narrative (Fieldnote Extract 3.13) describes that visit, prompted as an option to keep the caravan together when one car had been delayed in Belgium, while our car had already passed Madrid:

Fieldnote extract 3.13 Narrative: Granada

We heard from Souad and Brahim during the course of the day, that they had finally departed (along with Brahim's father, mother, brother and two-year-old niece). It would be impossible for them to catch us up at this point; but then the suggestion floated from somewhere: let's stop at Granada to see the Alhambra. Malika had been previously, as had Walid only last year (he said, you think your sister let us stop here without making me see it?) Abdelhakim and Zohra had never been. After some reassurance that it would be simple to find a cheap hotel (Malika knew one) and park the car somewhere safe, it was agreed.

We arrived in time to get an afternoon visiting ticket, parked the cars near the monument and entered with a few hours left to see it. We wandered through the different rooms and courtyards with other tourists, and it struck me that our group was one of the few who was reading the calligraphy inscriptions.

Abdelhakim and Zohra asked me to take a few pictures of them together. We took a group picture in the requisite spot, on the rampart overlooking the Albaycine and the valley.

Later that evening, after a nap at the hotel, we walked up to the viewpoint at the top of the Albaycine, where we happened upon the mosque of Granada. Abdelhakim took the opportunity to pray at sunset, while Zohra, Malika and I sat in the square with cold drinks.

We continued on early the next morning, but without Walid's group who had left already. Souad and Brahim were approaching as we continued towards the southern Spanish coast. Dragging our feet in order to give them time to catch up, we stopped to wander around and eat a seafood lunch in Marbella. I had the feeling with Zohra and Abdelhakim that they had never taken such pleasure in the "getting there" of going to Morocco – although Zohra was always smiling, even in the cold in Belgium, Abdelhakim had a new lightness. Maybe this was because we were almost there.

As the city began to shut down after lunch, we made our way back to the car and Souad started trying to locate us from the highway. After searching up and down a few side streets, Malika spotted her niece out on the sidewalk, and we were reunited with the other two cars from our caravan. After resting a bit, but finding no café open where we could sit (maybe it was Sunday already?) we organized ourselves to continue driving.

As this moment demonstrates, a number of factors aligned for the older generation to make the decision to stop to tour. We were all adults and traveling with relatively inconspicuous cars, so the problems of controlling multiple children or keeping an overloaded vehicle protected from thieves did not apply. Moreover, the site itself had a value for this group: the Alhambra traces its origin to Islamic history connected to Morocco. Beyond simply an aesthetically interesting city or a beautiful coastline – which, as is often argued, can be easily found in Morocco – it is a unique heritage site.

This decision to tour, in the end, was serendipitous, instigated by interruptions to the trajectory of our caravan toward Morocco. It was an example of a practice of touring not normally done by the parent generation. In fact, Walid's daughter Fatiha B expressed her disappointment in Conversation 3.21 that her parents had decided to visit the Alhambra the one year she didn't travel with them:

Conversation 3.21 Vacation without me

Fatiha, Antwerp, 5 March 2008, 50sec		
1	F	another reason why I didn't go was- because/ well,- (1.0) in=Mo**roc**co, it's always the same/ so- I- (.) **that year** I was (.6) um: (.9) well, absolutely **sure** I wouldn't **miss** anything, (.6) but- (.3) then eventually I **did** miss a couple of things, because it was the first time my parents went to Granada,=hheh and stayed for two day:s, (.4 .h) so:: that was (.5) a bit of a pity though. heheheh=yeah (.5) since I'm the only one who speaks Spanish, **yes**/ that was =hh=definitely=hh=hard/ .hh
2	LW	um so wai- um (.7) so they stopped in Granada on the way down? [or
3	F	[.h uh (.6) **yeah** (.) well/ on their way to Morocco
4	LW	that- that's so- that's not (.) **fair,**
5	F	yeah I **know**/ it was the first time I didn't go with them/ to Morocco and it was also the first time they (.) stopped there, and had a bit of a vacation (.7 .h) beforehand hhahh, before going to Morocco .hhh

Interestingly, Fatiha refers to the stop as "a bit of vacation beforehand" (5), underlining the normal single-minded trajectory of the journey, and the fact that this stop – perhaps in contrast to how she experiences Morocco – was a vacation. Though going to Morocco is also felt to be a vacation by some ("Attachments: Habitual Mobilities"), there are evidently ways that some feel it is not a vacation, at least not in the way that doing something like "touring the Alhambra" is. For many DVs in her generation, looking out the window along the drive to Morocco is not sufficient to satisfy the desire to see other places, but abandoning Morocco altogether is not preferable either. Becoming a 'tourist' along the way, or taking vacation elsewhere in alternating trips to Morocco, can be a way to balance maintaining attachment to Morocco and exploring elsewhere.

xvii Insulations: Flirting

A 'real' vacation, for many independent adults, also comes with romantic possibilities ("Embodiments: Diasporic, Touristic, Citizens"). Sexuality enters into tourist/host dynamics as part of the economic and power relationship between travelers and those who welcome them – for 'general' travelers as well as for diasporic ones (Panagakos 2016). For DVs in Morocco, romantic encounters are likewise integral to their holiday experience, through flirting, picking up, chatting up, or *la drague*. As the examples discussed here show, as much as these encounters are key to an affective atmosphere of being 'on holiday,' they also feed into viscous social and geographical networks that help DVs "keep amongst themselves" ("Insulations: Viscous Places of Protection"). In other words, insular spaces for romantic activity are made possible by their collective, viscous occupation of exclusive leisure spaces ("Insulations: Viscous Places of Consumption") and the common backgrounds and trajectories many of these individuals share as diasporic members of Moroccan families, visiting Morocco for summer vacation.

Unlike the stereotypical sexual encounter in a touristic holiday, these encounters are not presumptively temporary. As much as these can be *petits romances*, or brief encounters, they can become serious relationships. As Said attested, even chance encounters on vacation can lead to marriage. His wife

Figure 3.19 Nighttime flirtation, Meknes. French women speaking to the driver of a car with French plates.

is, like him, *française d'origine marocaine*. She comes from his same home-town in Morocco, where, 'happily,' they met on the beach one summer:

> bah disons=heureusement=donc on s'est rencontré à Tiznit, on=avait=pu
> pas=s- on=n'avait=pas=pu=se=rencontrer en France, puisque on n'était
> pas de la même eh: (.7) la même région, et:: eh/ on s'est rencontré là-bas
> well let's=say=happily=so we met in Tiznit, we=could=have=not- we=
> couldn't=have=met in France, since we're not from the same eh: (.7) the same
> region, and:: eh/ we met there

Yet, the openness to fortuitous romantic encounters can have insular borders. When I had asked Said, previously in this conversation, about possibly marrying a 'Moroccan,' he replied that they would be 'too different;' that they would be culturally distinct from each other. In that context, for him, 'a Moroccan' meant someone from Morocco, rather than someone who was from a Moroccan background, like his wife. Similarly, Noura ("Insulations: Viscous Places of Protection") characterized the flirtatious behavior of locally resident men as disrespectful, a product of a Moroccan 'mentality' ("Insulations: Mentality and Distrust"). In these perspectives, part of the assumption about romance that can develop in Morocco is that it is between DV men and women[5] who share the practice of being 'on holiday.'

Given the insulating dynamics of DV holiday practices, Said's happy first encounter with his wife was not entirely random. Being DVs on holiday to the same hometown created conditions of possibility that enabled it. As much as flirting can be part of the 'touristic' consumption of Morocco as a place for fun, it is also a potentially serious side of *insha'allah*, in which insulating leisure practices put appropriate partners in the same viscous spaces to meet each other over the summer. The examples recounted next (Figure 3.20; Fieldnote Extracts 3.14 and 3.15), in which I witnessed DVs flirting with each other, demonstrate how insulating forces like 'mentality,' economic power, and familiarity with diasporic reference points across Europe and Morocco play a role in how flirtations can succeed and fail.

Finding common trajectories

Places like aquatic parks seem to be prime pickup spots for DVs, with some encounters evolving more successfully than others. The notes from my first visit to Oasiria, an aquatic park in Marrakech, are filled with observations of visible public flirtations, plus a long flirtation between French-speaking Belgian Sanae and a French *kharij* firefighter:

Fieldnote extract 3.14 Sanae at Oasiria, 7 August 2008

Then, to oasiria, which was decidedly full of kharij. this is where all the NL plates go during the day.

Watched one group of 3 in wave pool, posturing: doing pushups, holding each other's heads underwater (maybe mid-twenties...) and then trying to chat up French 2 girls sitting chatting in front of them. the girls ignored, he tried maybe 3–4 times to get a name or anything.

Saw lots of other draguer occasions, including Sanae up close, with Yacine the pompier [firefighter] who started keeping us company while waiting for the navette that never comes.

v. interesting that a lot of his drague was sort of recognition thru kharijness – where in europe are you from, where in Morocco; taza, hoceima and linguistic similarities; local knowledges like roads from one place to another, and things that have been changed recently or not. she admits the problem of not being able to Not be bothered by men, which he takes as possibly a veiled refutation, but she doesn't mean him. he's impressed she came to learn arabic ...

to the point of trying to stay with us and not leave with his friends...

As I remarked in these fieldnotes, part of what makes these flirtations successful (in some cases) are the easy similarities to discover among DVs. Yacine's approach was much more subtle than some of the other *drageurs*

Figure 3.20 Flirting in Oasiria.

I witnessed that day. He was helped by circumstances, as we were all stuck waiting for the free bus between the aquatic park and the city center, giving him a chance to approach slowly. Once the linguistic barrier is passed (as Fred was not able to do with Naima in Fieldnote Extract 3.15), many DVs have similar dynamics of homes and displacements. Sanae and Yacine could find commonalities in their family histories and recognize the same homeplace geographies in Morocco and in Europe. They could even establish affiliative stance about the overaggressiveness of (some) men. All of these attributes signal their 'DV-ness' to each other, as much as their embodiment does through their co-presence at Oasiria that day in August, their clothing, and their accents in French. The insularity of these spaces is produced by such practices and interactions that make Oasiria become known as a place for DVs to go to find each other.

To successfully maintain a conversation beyond the initial greeting line, as Yacine did, the instigator must find commonalities. This process can be complicated by the multiplicity of Moroccan migration: no single background, language, or region in Morocco or in Europe is necessarily common between two DVs who meet coincidentally in Morocco. This problem materialized when I went with Naima, a Flemish-speaking Belgian, to Oasiria one afternoon.

Fieldnote extract 3.15 Naima at Oasiria, 9 August 2008

(After lunch) I went straight to Oasiria to meet Naima…

she talks like she doesn't like the annoying drageurs, but she is nonetheless very very careful about her appearance and tenue:

she wouldn't take off her shorts, saying her legs are fat (which I find hard to believe – a decidedly ideal figure). she has very striking eyes, hair, and a deep tan skin color that make her noticeable from afar. and she is noticed, and she knows that they notice, but she refuses to consider any of them. Sometimes, when they are particularly persistent, she replies in the repartee, but not always. She complains about them, the f*ckers, but I think she enjoys the attention. Constantly checking her phone, both of them [Belgian and Moroccan]!

For example, 'Fred' who came up to talk to her:

- Salam, es-tu instable ou c'est l'eau qui ne te conviens pas? [Hello, are you unstable or is it the water you don't like?]
- quoi? [what?]
- es-tu instable ou c'est l'eau qui ne te conviens pas? [are you unstable, or is it the water you don't like?]
- (shrug, turn away)
- c'est de l'humour [it's humor]

- quoi!??! (louder) [what!??!]
- c'est de l'humour l'HUMOUR [it's humor HUMOR]
- l'humour? [humor?]
- tu parles francais? kathederi bl arabiya? [you speak French? do you speak Arabic?]
- no non
- desolee, sorry
- bye (go away)

(the version he wrote down was somewhat more polite...)

it seems like la drague always happens in french – no matter who is on either end.

he came back by after she had gone off to deal with her hair to try to get info about her out of me, and we chatted for a while about his travel.

Naima's encounter with Fred (a DV from France) in Oasiria was exemplary of these kinds of encounters in a number of ways. Initially, her attitude toward being 'picked up' was typical of most women I witnessed: reject immediately. I remarked a few times in the fieldnotes on my impression that she wanted to be looked at, a judgment I made based on the attention she gave to her appearance, to arranging herself on the grass, as well as to her attire, changing clothes three times while we were there.

Yet she spent a lot of time telling me how annoying the boys are, how much she doesn't want to be bothered. She demonstrated that preference when Fred approached in her attitude and bodily orientation toward him. The interaction was complicated more so by the fact that he began in French, a language in which she seemed to have only rough competence, and so his attempt at 'humor' was an immediate failure. He then switched to *derija*, which also was a failed move because she is from an Amazigh family. Even later, when he came back while she was away from our spot to ask for my help in being introduced to her, he could not make any progress.[6] While some chance encounters, like Sanae's, seem to build on the likelihood of similar life histories among DVs, Fred's attempt to find those commonalities missed the target.

Viscosity on the street

Flirting encounters are enabled by spaces like Oasiria, but they might take place in any of the spaces DVs take part in during the summer – even on a public street. When Najat A and her older sister Slama A were out shopping for purses with Chaima, a cousin who was friends with Najat, I audio-recorded an instance of flirtation (Wagner 2017a). All three women were engaged looking at bags when a *draguer* – one of a group of unfamiliar DV men – called out the name of Najat and Slama's hometown as Najat paused in her shopping talk.

Most impressively, he identified it correctly – possibly recognizing them from France or having heard Najat speak and recognizing her accent. She did not respond to him; rather, she laughingly echoed his guess to her companions, probably toward her peer-aged cousin Chaima. Her repetition acknowledges that she heard him and is aware of his presence, but does not address him directly. The *draguer* continued by mentioning other towns in France about 100 kilometers from her hometown, possibly identifying this area as his French hometown. Still, neither Najat nor any of the other women addressed him directly; they finished their unsuccessful search through this vendor's available purses, then all three women initiated their departure down the street.

After waiting nearly two minutes from his last attempt for any verbal response from this group, the *draguer* continued: he wished them a nice holiday, to which both Najat and Chaima reply with thanks, and "you too." He then offered his number to one of them – probably Najat, as she replied by pushing her cousin Chaima to talk. Chaima is laughing at this point, and may have said something, though nothing is audible in the recording. Najat makes an excuse that she is with her big sister (Slama) and therefore not talking. In this same moment, she pushes her cousin twice to speak for herself. Nothing further is audible from the *draguer* as they walk away.

Once he is out of earshot, Najat addressed her cousin again, asking if in fact she was interested in these guys. Chaima replied negatively that it "wasn't her style," and then again with more detail, but inaudibly in the recording. Judging from Najat's final comment, telling her cousin she should have "checked out one of the friends," Chaima may have expressed an interest in another member of the group apart from the one who was speaking to them.

While this instance of flirting does not take place in an insulated site of viscous DV consumption, it does occur in a common site for DV leisure outings – the market in the old city center. It demonstrates how, even in public space, flirting is an insulating practice of being on holiday. The *draguer* knew how to get Najat's attention, by finding commonality in their place of origin. He can recognize her as a DV on the street, perhaps through her style of dress, her accent, the group of women with whom she walked, and other indescribable embodied attributes. Likewise, Najat knows how to respond, to encourage or discourage him, to give an acceptable excuse like familial propriety. Yet, her rejection is not out of hand: she passes the advance to her cousin, another DV who is similarly positioned to accept or reject this flirtation. Moreover, the women discuss strategy after the fact, what Chaima 'should have' done, possibly leading to what she will do next time.

These kinds of encounters may seem superficially frivolous, but they serve to reinforce the insular viscosity of DV vacation. As such practices assemble into the viscosity of how DVs take part in public spaces, the search for appropriate partners while engaging in leisure in Morocco is potentially quite consequential. Tradition in Morocco encourages finding a suitable partner and committing to marriage relatively quickly, without cohabitation or any unsupervised contact that would put in question the virginity of the bride. Stories told to me about an archetypal marriage framed it as springing from a single sighting of the woman by the man – as is the case with some of these flirtations – who then speaks to her parents.

Yet these examples indicate that only the approach of certain strangers, under certain conditions of propriety, is acceptable. The ways that DV bodies tend to stick together in certain places, to be visible and open for encounter among each other, contribute to producing these encounters and their aftereffects ("Embodiments: Having a Car"). While doing their own kind of tourism, their bodies are displayed to others, but in principle only the 'right kind' of others. Many processes in assemblage contribute to making these flirtations and marriages possible. Gendered access to autonomous movement and gender sensitivity of certain public spaces guide women to consume some places and not others, with certain barriers of protection and not others ("Insulations: A Typical Day"; "Insulations: Viscous Places of Protection"). Enclosed, exclusive places like Oasiria create an environment that is at once safe and full of potential encounters. Embodiment, both in body and in language, also plays a part, enabling DVs to recognize each other even in uninsulated spaces. Yet viscous spatial insulation from resident Moroccans enables them to meet each other in places that combine a gendered 'respect' with their purposeful pursuit of leisure. They can fulfill the project of 'getting out' and find others who are doing likewise, escaping boredom ("Embodiments: Gendered Boredom") and pursuing the "sun, sand, sea, and sex" of a touristic holiday.

xviii Embodiments: Suntanning

Seeking the sun is a classic form of embodied activity that motivates leisure travelers to depart. In a material sense, sun interacts with bodies in specific ways: sun heats, making bodies sweat, and/or try to cool themselves; and sun shines, making skin change color following its pigmentation, from light to dark, dark to darker, or pale to red. These material changes are part of the ways that tourists embody 'doing tourism,' in assemblage with the sun. The ways they do this reflect autonomy to spend their earned labor capital for embodied leisure capital, in that they are not obligated to withstand the sun in order to survive but choose to partake of it as a form of leisure consumption. It also reflects how the sun interacts with human bodies: by warming them up and causing their skin to tan. Both of these embodiments play a role in how DVs experience their vacation in Morocco.

Recognizing that the sun has material effects on the body is central to reflecting on why the sun is widely seen as dangerous in Morocco. Speaking from ethnographic experience, much informal health advice I received over my time spent in Morocco was focused on maintaining a balanced body temperature, not to become too hot or too cold or fluctuate too quickly between the two. I was instructed, for example, to avoid sitting too long in the sun, because it causes dizziness, headaches, or worse. The sun can also be blamed for causing the flu, because sitting outside and overheating is too quickly reversed by coming inside to the cold.

Yet for visitors from colder climates, like Mohammed and his student organization – predominantly composed of Moroccan-origin Dutch university students – who chose Marrakech as their 'fun' trip of the year, this kind of fluctuation is transposed to a broader timescale: one wants to absorb as much sun as possible in the warm months in order to survive the colder ones. When I asked him "Why Marrakech?" as their group destination, Mohammed replied,

> why not? [hhehehehe .he why Marrakech. (1.1) Marrekech eh it's a nice city, (.) a lot of::(.5) the group- a lot of eh: members of the group, (.) have never been in Marrakech so it was now the: the **chance** to be here, (.3) and (.3) we thought why not? (1.4) it's a nice city, a lot of: culture, (1.2) and the: (.4) and the **sun**'s here

For this group, as they were on a leisure trip, Marrakech presented a possibility to tour elsewhere ("Attachments: Touring Elsewhere") and become familiar with their own country ("Attachments: The Nostalgia of 'Home'") as much as to get to absorb and enjoy some sun.

The sun can also have negative effects for DVs, who might suffer in heat to which their bodies are unaccustomed. Because of their autonomous economic mobility, however, they have ample means to escape it.

Fieldnote extract 3.16 Compilation: Effects of heat

– 7 August 2008: lunch in Marrakech with a family – husband, wife, two children, and the husband's younger sister – from the Netherlands, just before they departed for the airport. We sat at an inexpensive restaurant on the main square, Djemaa el Fna, in the middle of a hot summer day. While the two parents ate, and fed their two children, the adult sister complained throughout the meal of the heat: she couldn't eat anything heavier than a salad, and barely that. Instead, she said, she would get a sandwich in the air conditioning at the airport.

– 10 August 2008: Out with the group from Belgium, three guys and Naima, plus her younger sister with us today. The guys want to walk through the souk, even though it's the middle of the day and blisteringly hot, so Naima is dragging her feet and trying to entice them to go to a pool instead. She keeps coming up to me and practicing her French, complaining that she only wants to swim, to cool off, to tan.

These examples reflect both how some DVs were seeking the sun and how being exposed to the sun and its heat becomes a significant embodied experience during visits in Morocco. It can become overpowering, killing one's appetite, or can differentiate between leisure activities, like shopping in the hot marketplace versus swimming.

Naima's desire to return to the pool fit directly into touristic practices of enjoying the sun. Tanning practices play out in a dance between heating and cooling the body – enjoying the heat of the sun alternately with the cool of water. For many DVs, this dynamic is the only way to survive the heat of Moroccan summers. While sitting by a hotel pool in Fes ("Insulations: Familial Obligations"; "Attachments: Resisting Pressure"), Mounir commented that he could not imagine surviving the heat without going to a pool. Part of his privileged position, in being on holiday, is that he is not obligated to labor in that weather, as are many resident Moroccans. In being a leisure consumer, he can choose to imbibe of heat by sitting in the sun, because he has the option of cooling off by jumping in the water, or at its extreme by returning to France.

Inasmuch as DVs tend to seek the sun, their frequent preference for sunbathing is complicated by contrasting ideologies of tanned skin in Morocco. Dyer (1997, 49) comments on tanning as a phenomenon specific to (white) women of the twentieth century, for whom tanning comes to symbolize leisure and travel. Previously, he claims (1997, 49–50), tanning was associated with outdoor labor activity, making it a symbol of the inverse of (white) leisure, unrelenting work in a harsh sun. This resonates to some extent in Morocco, but not universally. Resident Moroccans may choose to tan, but this choice is likely linked with differing ideas of social class and prestige reflected in skin tone.

Many DVs encounter this ideological difference in the most direct way, as a difference in preference between themselves and the resident Moroccans they interact with on a daily basis. Jamila B. reported as much in Conversation 3.22:

Conversation 3.22 They don't go to the beach

Jamila, Den Haag, 12 April 2008, 50sec		
1	LW	do you go with them ((resident family)) (.) to the beach? or
2	J	did we em:: (.4) no. (2.0) [**they don't go** to the beach (.8) the family::/ our family. don't go to the beach
3	LW	[so
4	LW	are they older? or:: like (.) your age
5	J	they **don't like it,** they um:: (.8) uh:: (.6) they are afraid of the sun/ (.) they like to be uh:[: **white skin.**
6	LW	[wh- yea-
7	LW	Mmhmm
8	J	and that's the reason they don't like the beach/ and **we** like (.) make ahehhhe.h a brown skin, so
9	LW	yeah, that's- this is something everybody says
10	J	yeah?
11	LW	in Morocco they're always trying to make themselve[s whiter
12	J	[makes white yeah, and we hhehehe return from the beach we are f- we re- ((high pitch)) ohh what did you **do!** Hhahahaha

Jamila's attitude was echoed by every other participant who discussed this topic. Between DVs and resident Moroccans, there was a mutual lack of comprehension about the desire to tan or to whiten. Other DVs commented that they needed to be tan to look their best at a wedding or to impress their colleagues at work, when they return, with the depth of their tan. Like the beauty services acquired at the salon (Wagner 2017b), tanning is an element of physical capital inscribed on the body and acts like a souvenir as proof of leisure.

In that they are able to make the choice for the sun in Morocco rather than the cold of Europe, or to choose to tan their skin as a sign of leisure consumption, DVs practice this embodied mode of their visits to Morocco touristically. They have access to capital which enables them to move in and out of the sun, absorbing what their bodies want and escaping when their bodies are uncomfortable. Hence, it is no surprise that the practice of tanning is a point of intense distinction between DVs and resident Moroccans: as a reflection of their leisure and class, and their mobility between Morocco and elsewhere, absorbing the sun for pleasure materializes the difference between visiting Morocco and living there into their bodies.

xix Insulations: Hypermobile viscosity

The melodic refrain of "American Boy" by Estelle is part of the fabric of the summer of 2008: on the car radio while driving for the sake of driving, at night in Fes after the air has cooled down from the daytime heat.

Fieldnote extract 3.17 Narrative: Escaping in Fes

Driving with Noura and her two friends in the orange Kia she rented, as she tells the story of how the (Moroccan) rental company was inefficient and unreliable from the moment she arrived. She wasn't meant to have a Kia at all, but some other more substantial car.

We are just one car in the caravan of three, all French Moroccans except one Algerian, moving from café to restaurant, then to another café, then back to the one where we started out. Each move seems to be driven by the pull of group action: a desire emerges from one member to eat something, and soon we are all motivated from our café table to the road, debating which restaurant (of the choice of three or four they know and like) to head for; then we are stalled standing by the cars, as two members are off in deep, heated discussion about some personal issue that never becomes clear to me; one of the waiting five breaks off, jumps in a taxi out of boredom and impatience, and then we are all motivated to follow him to the restaurant he chose. Once we arrive there, he is nowhere to be found. He wandered down the street to one of the other options (out of the four), but they were there last night so no one wants to join him, and he is pulled back to us. An hour has passed from the first movement to sitting down, and by now the kitchen is practically closed, and we have to convince the waiter (with some darija codeswitching) to find us something to eat.

This process revolves, repeats, shaping the evening into something different, where new and old things happen as the movement changes, yet the same as the previous one in which so much nothing happened. In the end, it is 4 AM when I can't keep up out of exhaustion. We are in the Kia, riding in a caravan, with radios loud and momentary streaks of speed to chase each other on the empty boulevards of the former French city of Fes, when we come across a wedding party doing essentially the same thing – celebrating the end of the night by riding around city in caravan, horns blaring to announce the new couple, and our three cars momentarily join theirs around a traffic circle before we take off in a different direction. It feels like I'm in high school again, with the headiness of unhindered mobility and late night thrill-seeking, trying to wake the neighbors and see dawn.

Being distinctive and autonomous modes of travel, cars contribute to the affect of being 'at leisure.' Sheller elicits the 'aesthetic, emotional and sensory responses to driving' (2004: 222) that are intensively embedded in car consumption. They become implicated in tropes of independence, speed, and escape, particularly in contexts where cars provide opposition to regimented daily life (Garvey 2001). As extensions of bodies, the 'driver-car' (Dant 2004) becomes part of the potential field of movement and form of taking up space through an extended embodiment. Moreover, they reconfigure sensory experiences of space, like the city (Thrift 2004) or the nation (Edensor 2004). Cars and the ways they are used by DVs in Morocco reflect this capacity for taking pleasure in speed, freedom, and the status of hypermobile consumption, as they speed around their hometowns and across the country. Such hypermobile leisure practices of DV drivers and cars in Morocco create an insulating space for them to take pleasure in consuming what they find enjoyable in Morocco while sticking together as a group.

I call these practices 'hypermobile' because their purpose seems to be mobility itself: movement for the sake of movement. As related in the Fieldnote Extract 3.17 narrative, our group that night was engaging in consumption activities like drinking and eating in cafés and restaurants, but also going around the city to feel the speed and freedom of movement. These movements are part of the intense spontaneity of *insha'llah*, which also insulates how DVs experience Morocco on holiday. They are familiar with Morocco geographically and socially: with the services available, the 'savings' assured by their European ability to spend, and their 'Moroccan' ability to communicate. By being embedded in viscous networks of DV geographies, they find other DV friends to take part in leisure with them. Regarding this group, Noura told me they did not often meet in France but found each other nearly every year in Morocco. Though they came from different places in France, they became interlinked through mutual acquaintance, diasporic homes in proximity to each other, and coincidental timing. Their shared mobility experiences – and the speeds with which they are communally able to move – make them into a group.

The importance of hypermobility as a DV leisure practice becomes more evident through comparison between mobility experiences and practices. While Noura, with her own rented Kia, was easily integrated into those activities, the example in Fieldnote Extract 3.18 of Najat, with no car of her own, shows in contrast the effort needed to join in those insular, hypermobile viscous spaces.

Hypermobile without a car

For Najat A., perhaps more blatantly than many other participants I hung out with, access to a car was a potent problem. On the evening she, her cousin Chaima, and I went for a night out, automobility became relevant along multiple dimensions: from our ability to be mobile to reach the right consumption spaces, to Najat's need for gendered insulation and protection from masculine dangers.

Fieldnote extract 3.18 Nighttime movements around Meknes, 16 August 2008

cars cars cars: drague from cars, or hiding from it in a car. I'm feeling here the force of lack of car mobility on what Najat manages to do: yes we can get places by taxi, but it makes us a bit more vulnerable to things like catcalls, slowness, splitting up a group... she still frequents the same car-places but she has to mobilize in a different way to arrive. To go out to Aladdin (whose pronunciation baffled me until I saw the sign – /aladi~/ instead of /aladin/) we have to call the taxi driver she knows to come get us, and pay him extra for having come a long way at our request. Practically running from the house, partially because we're late, partially (i think) to avoid the crowd of men who are in the café we pass, and the whistles that follow us in Najat's short skirt and Chaima's little black dress. happily, the taxi is waiting.

On the way, N wants to get a recharge for her phone...

we pull up by a phone place just past bab elmansour but she hesitates to get out, asking Ch to go with her, then ending up with me going to get it. there are crowds of idle men on the street, and anything that came out of the taxi would be harassed but her probably more because of the miniskirt. the protection of the car is palpable – it's a mobile curtain between her and the surrounding men.

All the places we go are distant, car places: Aladdin on the old road to fes, Dalia out near the marjane. not places you accidentally come across, places you have to make an effort in a vehicle to achieve. @ Aladdin, Ch's cousin Yacine comments on this: she says we came by taxi and his reaction is condoling, or slightly disbelieving: you will have a hard time leaving then…but no, we have the phone number for the taxi, we can call him.

On the way to Aladdin, another example of car issues: we pass a car which N says is [male friend]'s car, stopped by police. we're all sure that he hasn't actually done anything wrong, it's just for the bribe…

…

Music stops at 1:20, and it's unclear if the place is closed or just unanimated. the boys with us leave all together and we are left vulnerable: the guys at the next table immediately start, inviting us to join them which prompts Ch to stand up like we're going somewhere, but we pull her back down. soon it seems clear that there's no point in staying, but we don't feel like going home… outside, the taxi is loyally waiting for us.

Start home, but talk to [male friend] midway and change course for Dalia [a nightclub in a distant hotel]. Ch says, on va pas rentrer en boite [we're not going back in a nightclub], which makes the irony of our position totally clear: don't want to go home but there's nowhere else to stay 'tranquil'.

N gives the driver a 100 and essentially says give me whatever change you think is correct. (i think she paid 70 for each trip)

Arriving at Dalia it's another man trap: hordes by the door at the right, so we ask driver to take us left, and we sit in the car waiting for [male friend] to arrive. A car arrives which N takes to be his, so we all get out; it wasn't. but our taxi leaves so we are stuck waiting in the cold. he arrives a moment later, turning left instead of right, and N calls him to tell him we are on the other side.

Coming over this way, his friends exit the car and enter the club; we get in his tight, overdone convertible with his little local cousin (what is he doing in the car anyway?) he takes us home…

Our night out began at Aladdin, an entertainment complex on the edge of Meknes (Figure 3.21). It was unlike the nightclubs I had seen in Marrakech or Casablanca in that the admission price was the cost of one drink – 25 dirham – and alcohol was not served. In fact, it had almost a family atmosphere – I commented in my fieldnotes (not cited in Fieldnote Extract 3.18) that the atmosphere was "like a wedding with no bride or groom," as there

Figure 3.21 Aladdin, outside of Meknes. 17 August 2008, 12:40 am.

were mothers with their children as well as other young women veiled and unveiled, and teenagers and young men playing billiards and smoking shisha.

Aladdin (Figure 3.21) is positioned remotely in terms of the city's social geography, on a road leading out of town, by which taxi traffic does not pass very frequently. Its geographical position puts it among other car-accessible places that are purposefully at some distance from more populated areas of the city, making them more difficult to reach without automobility. In my notes, Yacine pitied us for being without transport, and the process of going to and coming from was expensive and difficult because of our transport handicap. We managed to get there and leave reasonably efficiently because Najat knew to negotiate transportation in advance. She had her taxi waiting when we left the house, and again waiting when we were ready to leave, effectively hiring a chauffeur for the evening. The ample parking available there, and the dearth of taxis when we walked out, seem to reinforce that it is the kind of place one goes to with transportation assured.

Our taxi substitutes for having our own car, both to transport us to Aladdin and back, and to enable Najat to leave the house and be protected. As a young, attractive woman, dressed for going out, there are men she does not want to see her – men on the street, men watching from cafés, men whom she cannot trust to leave her in peace. In the terms that Noura laid out ("Insulations: Viscous Places of Protection"), discussing 'respectful' places where DV women feel that they won't be approached aggressively, the car becomes a conduit, providing a protective bubble transporting her body between nodes of viscosity.

Najat was in need of this insulation three times during this evening. First, as we left her house and were forced to walk past the men in the café, they did not let our passage go unnoticed. Second, when we stopped for her to buy credit for her phone, she was unable even to get out of the car because of the certainty that she would be followed by catcalls on the street. This street was a central axis in Meknes, cutting through the old city and quite busy even at that late hour, but the (male) crowdedness made attention to her appearance more likely instead of less.[7] Finally, when we moved a second time, from Aladdin to the entrance of a nightclub at Hotel Dalia, we were left without any cover but the taxi itself from the men hanging out around the entrance. While the interiors of these places might afford protection against undesired gazes, the only protection on the exterior is inside a car. Once we were out of the car, standing vulnerable in the parking lot, Najat telephoned her friend to tell him to drive to us rather than walk past the entrance to where we knew his car was sitting.

As much as Najat needed the car to protect herself, she needed to protect herself because she wanted to go out to car-accessible places. She could have gone other places by foot or by taxi. She could stay at her neighbor's house to chat, or easily go to the central old city or other nearby places. Her consumption desires, however, are linked with hypermobility, as it is being practiced by her friends and acquaintances who were themselves also moving around Meknes that day. Most of her energy was devoted to getting out of the house to enjoy herself, to see friends, and to experience her own leisure. On this day alone, we had been out of the house for three separate consumption events: first out to the swimming pool, then out to the city around dinnertime, then again out to 'go out.' Being without her own car presented a significant problem for her. She had to manage her mobility by finding taxis or finding rides to get to the places other DVs frequent by private vehicle.

All of these parts are interacting in the hypermobile dynamic of DVs moving at will in Morocco. Without a car, Najat found it sometimes difficult to keep up with other DVs in their activities. She managed by having a contact, a trusted taxi driver who works at night, whom she knows she can call when she is stuck. Yet that does not mean she does not run the risk of being immobile: if he does not answer the phone, is occupied, or is not working that evening, she is again left without transport. This was nearly the case at the end of the evening. When we arrived at Hotel Dalia, we waited in the taxi for Najat's friend who she wanted to meet. Thinking she saw his car, we all exited the taxi so he could leave, but she was mistaken. We spent a few minutes literally outside in the cold, not wanting to enter the nightclub but with the possibility of neither protection nor mobility until her friend arrived.

Hypermobility thus becomes part of what keeps these viscous geographies sticking together and repels entities that cannot fit into its parameters. Noura and her gang made a path around Fes that night, as they had done for numerous other nights around and outside of Fes, that cannot be tracked without being similarly mobile. Najat and Chaima struggled to keep up with others, making arrangements to be able to meet at the right place and the right time, and managing their mobility in between. I, as well, discovered new spaces of DV leisure and interaction by following along in their journeys – for which I am reliant upon accessing their same mobilities. I also found myself getting stuck when, without my own car, I could not keep up. Each of these practices latches onto flows of hypermobile viscosity of DV leisure consumption as it moves collectively from one site to the next throughout the summer.

Left out

While hypermobility may seem distinctively 'touristic' as a practice, skimming the surface and stopping at sites of consumption, it is not exclusively a DV practice: the silent voices in these stories are the resident Moroccan families who may have been left behind disappointed while their cousins go out. These family members are sometimes 'taken along' as participants, but their participation is uncertain. An example is in Najat's story: her friend arrived to get us from Hotel Dalia with a young cousin as his passenger, too young to be entering a nightclub. It seemed like the boy had just come along for the ride, soon to be dropped off before the driver would go out again. Other examples came up like a cousin who was brought along to the beach or an aunt who was always around during the holiday ("Insulations: Familial Obligations"), sometimes with obvious pleasure for all parties and other times with mixed feelings. Apart from the car mobility provided by their visiting families from Europe, they may not otherwise have an opportunity for 'going out' to locations and activities that require automobility.

One participant told me that these relationships with family who wait and hope for an outing are conflicting. The desire to please the family pulls for acquiescence, but once taken along in the car, this family member becomes a burden. He or she will have to be provided for and made to feel a welcome participant in whatever activities by the hosts, who are implicitly obliged to pay all their costs. The ways DVs consume, spending their money by comparing costs favorably to EU prices, is usually unattainable for their locally resident families. It eventually becomes easier to avoid opening the car door to other family members, or to make specific decisions about who can accompany on what kinds of trips.

In that sense, hypermobility really does create an insulating boundary – not only between DVs and the general public but also between DVs and their families. Their speed and scope of mobility may not be accessible to members of their resident families, independent of their help. Through repetition of their consumption practices, they eventually make themselves inaccessible as they continue on leisure pursuits with no room for family to accompany them. For the most part, however, DVs do not abandon their families. Toward the end of my fieldwork, as the summer was ending and people began preparing for return, I found more and more participants excused themselves from meeting me because they were devoting the remaining days to visiting family.

Although it was frustrating as an ethnographer in the moment to have nothing to 'observe,' I can now observe that the hypermobility of the holiday is slowed down at some point to allow time to see family. Obviously, I was not invited to witness this, but that fact, in a sense, convinces me that these participants were doing what they said – going home to see family.

xx Insulations: Being stopped

At some point, the congregation of cars into Morocco reaches too great an intensity; the energetic hypermobility of having a car runs into barriers and blockages. The materiality of cars makes them visual extensions of DV embodiments ("Embodiments: Having a Car"), as well as objects that take up space, have accidents, move too fast, and impede each other's progress. DV cars become a sight on the side of the road (Stewart 1996), or a stopping that materially marks their presence in Morocco for themselves and for resident Moroccans. This last vignette documents how DVs, as they are embodied through their cars, are stopped, interrupted, and separated from other vehicles as they move around Morocco. Finally, we reverse the journey we started at the opening vignette – looking at how they slow traffic and congest the streets as they start on their way 'back home.'

Congestion

Like shop owners and taxi drivers who referred me to parking areas ("Embodiments: Having a Car"), other DVs sometimes commented on the presence or absence of cars. Sanae, who normally spends her time on the northern coast, remarked on how light the presence of DV cars was during her summer spent in Rabat. She was expecting at some point to see an influx of foreign cars, but it did not happen the same way as in Tangier (6 August 2008). Tangier, and other ports along the northern coast at Sebta, Al Hoceima, and Nador, are the frontier points where all EU cars must pass (and be counted), so naturally there is a higher concentration there before they disperse into the rest of Morocco. That higher concentration makes them visible blockages in northern roadways and creates material consequences.

Fieldnote extract 3.19 Tangier, 17 July 2008

Every time we go out on this day, we see an accident on the airport road going by their house. The one on the way back from coffee is the worst – 1 car flipped over, at least 2 others damaged on the other side of the road, and still clumps of people and police huddled around each other near the cars looking shocked and distressed. Brahim is talking to his father on the phone as we pass, and his father seems to ask where the cars are from, since Brahim replies that he can't see the license plates.

On this day, spent with Malika and her family in Tangier, automobile accidents were rampant. Their house was near the road leading from the center of Tangier to the airport, and on all of the three times we left the house that day we saw accidents on that road of varying severity, causing traffic backup in both directions. DV cars create temporary but stringent pressure on existing infrastructure that sometimes leads to the most extreme manifestation of being stopped: fatality. Brahim's father asks if Brahim can see the number plates on the fallen vehicles; his question evokes how the visibility of DVs through their cars is also a way of keeping track of friends and families, to see if "someone we know" is involved.

Accidents are one recognizable event at the side of the road. DV cars being stopped by police is another. Figure 3.22 shows a French car being stopped by police and the crowd that gathered to watch as the car's occupants and the police argued.

Driving with Brahim and Souad from Tangier to Ksar Sghir one day, we encountered a similar stoppage to the one pictured in Figure 3.22 on the return trip. As we left a village and rejoined the road back into the center of Tangier, we were coasting down a hill when we were stopped by the police. The children woke up, and all three of the adult passengers became somehow more still. Coming up to the window, the police asked for Brahim's

Figure 3.22 Crowd gathering as occupants of a French car argue with the police who stopped them. Castellejo (near border to Ceuta, Spain). 20 August 2008, 8 pm.

license and his customs certificate for the car, which he readily produced (along with, his wife later told me, 100 dirham (approximately 10 Euro) folded inside them). The police accused him of driving 10 kilometers over the speed limit, but Brahim pointed out that he was clocked, somewhat unfairly, while coming down a hill. He exited the car briefly and walked back toward the police car, then returned, and we drove off with everything apparently sorted.

Whether Brahim had exceeded the speed limit was not really an issue. The purpose of the stop was understood by everyone, including, as Souad later told me, another officer to whom Brahim spoke while he was out of the car, as a way of excising a bribe. He may have paid more of a bribe to the other officer; in any case, that officer released him without a ticket, and his papers were returned to him before he got back in the car.

Traffic stops like these are not uncommon. Driving on different roads, in different cities during the summer, it is normal to see cars stopped at certain points and notice that the number plate is foreign. Najat saw it on the way to Aladdin, and we knew what was going on: "we're all sure that he hasn't actually done anything wrong, it's just for the bribe" ("Insulations: Hypermobile Viscosity"). Fedwa and Amina's discussion about Fedwa's brother being stopped by the police ("Insulations: Mentality and Distrust") is another example of how DVs understand and react to being stopped. From their conversation, there is a sense of the understood unfairness of this system, but also their ability to surmount it. Fedwa's brother is not daunted by the police pressure; he responds appropriately but is resistant. She points out that the behavior of the police will not encourage DVs to return – precisely why the king discourages corruption. That said, some DVs see ways of using these police practices to their advantage. They can use their ability to bribe their way out of a ticket to break rules that, in Europe, would have much more severe penalties.

Yet DV automobiles seem to be a magnet for this kind of attention. Being in highly visible cars, marked by their number plates as well as by expensive makes and models, renders their extended embodiment an easy target for resident Moroccans to show resistance to their 'arrogance' and hypermobility by stopping them. Whether they follow the rules or not, their visibility and intense presence results, sometimes, in their being stopped.

Exit

That stopping is not necessarily an agentive process: it also happens in the way DV cars take up space in Morocco, creating radiating cumulative effects through their concentration and *viscosity*. The way they take up space potentially impacts individuals with whom they might never come in contact. As their cars pour into and pour out of Morocco, their added volume visibly and materially slows traffic to a standstill in some places for two months of the year.

Fieldnote extract 3.20 Stopped traffic, 21 August 2008

leaving Tangier on 21 august, and the traffic was noticeably thicker than when I looked before. took some pics with my phone by the port, but as I walked further down along the beach, more and more traffic, and finally police officers with a blockade in the middle of the road. They were preventing people from turning towards the port, asking drivers if they are musafrin [travelers] or not. I imagine they were using the *longeur* of the avenue as a way of controlling the queue, like an amusement park ride.

all of the arteries towards the port looked blocked – not stalled, but definitely slow.

At the very last turn, DV cars moving toward the port in Tangier cause miles of backup and cause the city to block off a major road – the main road that lines the waterfront along the bay – to provide some organization for the traffic (see Figures 3.23 and 3.24). They were turning away local drivers to find alternate routes, while they turned 'musafrin' – the DVs leaving Morocco,

Figure 3.23 Police redirecting traffic from the Avenue d'Espagne, Tangier.

Figure 3.24 Traffic for the Tangier port, Avenue d'Espagne, Tangier.

literally 'travelers' – into the queue. DV automotive presence may be more visible leaving than arriving: the cars exiting the ferry spread so quickly across Morocco that they may only block Tangier roads briefly, but the progress of departure on this particular day was so congested that the cars were undoubtedly blocking the road most of the day. The new port at Tangier Med, directly linked to motorways leading off in other directions, will change the dynamics of this entrance and exit. The presence of DVs, however, will still be felt through their automobility and the viscous movements of being stopped it creates at the side of the road.

Notes

1 See Lesthaeghe (2000), Manço (1999), and Ouali (2004) in relation to Belgium; Guénif Souilamas (2000), Lacoste-Dujardin (1992), Lepoutre (1997), Tribalat (1995, 1996) in relation to France; and de Boer (2009), Bos and Fritschy (2006), and Cottaar et al.(2009) in relation to the Netherlands.
2 See chapters in Bistolfi and Zabbal (1995), Césari and McLoughlin (2005), and Modood et al. (2006) for detailed discussions by country.
3 Until a 2004 set of laws regarding women's and family rights were signed by King Mohammed VI, citizenship could only be passed patrilineally. It is now passed by either Moroccan parent.
4 Due to copyright, I cannot reproduce the images here. See https://www.marhaba. fm5.ma/ for current examples.

5 Acknowledging, of course, that this dynamic is heteronormative. Homosexual flirtations were not something I directly observed in public spaces, though I may not be aware of the parameters through which it would happen.
6 When he came back, he discovered me writing down the course of their conversation. I explained my research to him, and he offered to write the conversation himself. I stayed loyal to Naima's evident preference and did not tell Fred anything about her.
7 Why could I get out of the car when they couldn't? Not only was I not dressed very provocatively, but the rules that apply to those perceived to be Moroccan are not the same to those perceived to be foreign. That said, would have been nice if the taxi driver had gone to get it.

References

Abu-Lughod, J.L. (1981). *Rabat: Urban apartheid in Morocco*. Princeton, NJ: Princeton University Press.
Abu-Lughod, L. (1986). *Veiled sentiments: Honor and poetry in a Bedouin society*. Berkeley: University of California Press.
Ahmed, S., Castañeda, C., Fortier, A-M., and Sheller, M. (Eds.). (2003). *Uprootings/ regroundings: Questions of home and migration*. New York; Oxford: Berg.
Aït Mous, F. (2011). Les enjeux de l'amazighité au Maroc. *Confluences Méditerranée*, *3*(78), 121–31.
Aitchison, C., Hopkins, P.E., and Kwan, M.P. (2007). *Geographies of Muslim identities: Diaspora, gender and belonging*. Aldershot: Ashgate.
Anderson, B. (2004). Time-stilled space-lowed: How boredom matters. *Geoforum*, *35*(6), 739–54.
Arnaut, K. (2012). Super-diversity: Elements of an emerging perspective. *Diversities*, *14*(2), 1–16.
Berger, J., and J. Mohr. 1989. *A Seventh Man: The Story of a Migrant Worker in Europe*. Cambridge: Granta Books, in association with Penguin Books.
Berriane, M., and Popp, H. (Eds.). (1999). *Le tourisme au Maghreb: Diversification du produit et développement local et régional* (Vol. Colloques et seminaires No 79). Tanger: la Faculté des Lettres et des Sciences Humaines – Rabat.
Bissell, D. (2010). Passenger mobilities: Affective atmospheres and the sociality of public transport. *Environment and Planning D: Society and Space*, *28*(2), 270–89.
Bistolfi, R., and Zabbal, F. (Eds.). (1995). *Islams d'Europe: Intégration ou insertion communautaire?* La Tour d'Aigues: Editions de l'Aube.
Blunt, A. (2005). Cultural geography: Cultural geographies of home. *Progress in Human Geography*, *29*(4), 505–15.
Bos, P., and W. Fritschy (eds). 2006. *Morocco and the Netherlands: Society, Economy, Culture*. Amsterdam: VU University Press.
Bourdieu, P. (1984). *Distinction: A social critique of the judgment of taste*. Cambridge, MA: Harvard University Press.
Brah, A. (1996). *Cartographies of diaspora: Contesting identities*. London: Routledge.
Brand, L. (2006). *Citizens abroad: Emigration and the state in the Middle East and North Africa*. Cambridge: Cambridge University Press.
Caletrío, J. (2014). "This is not me": Conspicuous consumption and travel aspirations of the European middle classes. In Birtchnell, T., and Caletrío, J. (Eds.). *Elite mobilities, changing mobilities*. Abingdon: Routledge, 194–208.

CCME. (n.d.). Le conseil de la communauté Marocaine à l'étranger | Présentation | Le Conseil. Retrieved 27 October 2010 from http://www.ccme.org.ma/fr/Le-Conseil/Pr%C3%A9sentation/Le-Conseil-de-la-communaut%C3%A9-marocaine-%C3%A0-l-%C3%A9tranger.html.

Césari, J. (1994). *Être musulman en France : Associations, militants et mosquées.* Paris: Karthala Editions.

Césari, J., and S. McLoughlin (eds). 2005. *European Muslims and the Secular State.* Aldershot: Ashgate.

Cohen, M.I., and Hahn, L. (1966). *Morocco: Old land, new nation.* London: Pall Mall Press.

Coleman, S., and Eade, J. (2004). *Reframing pilgrimage: Cultures in motion.* London: Routledge.

Conradson, D. (2003). Geographies of care: Spaces, practices, experiences. *Social & Cultural Geography*, *4*(4), 451–4.

Conway, D., and Potter, R.B. (Eds.). (2009). *Return migration of the next generations: 21st century transnational mobility.* Aldershot: Ashgate.

Crang, P. (1997). Performing the tourist product. In Rojek, C., and Urry, J. (Eds.). *Touring cultures.* London; New York: Routledge, 137–54.

Crick, M. (1989). Representations of international tourism in the social sciences: Sun, sex, sights, savings, and servility. *Annual Review of Anthropology*, *18*(1), 307–44.

Cottaar, Annemarie, Nadia Bouras, and Fatiha Laouikili. 2009. *Marokkanen in Nederland: De Pioniers Vertellen.* Amsterdam: Meulenhoff.

Dant, T. (2004). The driver-car. *Theory, Culture & Society*, *21*(4–5), 61–79.

Daoud, Z. (2011). *La diaspora Marocain en Europe.* Casa: La Croisée des Chemins.

de Boer, S. (2009). *Marokkaan in Nederland Hollander in Marokko.* Den Haag: Elmar.

de Haas, H. (2006). *Engaging diasporas: How governments and development agencies can support diaspora involvement in the development of origin countries (study for Oxfam Novib).* Oxford: University of Oxford; International Migration Institute.

———. (2007). Morocco's migration experience: A transitional perspective. *International Migration*, *45*(4), 39–70.

de Haas, H., and Vezzoli, S. (2010). *Migration and development: Lessons from the Mexico-US and Morocco-EU experiences* (Working paper No. 22). Oxford: International Migration Institute.

de Mas, P. (1978). *Marges marocaines: Limites de la coopération au développement dans une région périphérique.* The Hague: NUFFIC/IMWOO/Projet Remplod.

Driessen, H. (1998). The 'new immigration' and the transformation of the European–African frontier. In Wilson, T.M., and Donnan, H. (Eds.). *Border identities: Nation and state at international frontiers.* Cambridge: Cambridge University Press, 96–116.

Duval, D.T. (2003). When hosts become guests: Return visits and diasporic identities in a Commonwealth eastern Caribbean community. *Current Issues in Tourism*, *6*(4), 267–308.

Dyer, R. (1997). *White.* London: Routledge.

Edensor, T. (2004). Automobility and national identity: Representation, geography and driving practice. *Theory Culture & Society*, *21*(4–5), 101–20.

England, K. (2010). Home, work and the shifting geographies of care. *Ethics, Place & Environment*, *13*(2), 131–50.

Ennaji, M. (2010). L'équilibre de La Distance L'autre, Une Curiosité. In Dahan, P., and Lausberg, S. (Eds.). *Le Maroc et l'Europe: Six Siècles Dans Le Regard de l'autre*. Brussels: Somogy, 72–85.

Ferrer-Gallardo, X. (2008). The Spanish–Moroccan border complex: Processes of geopolitical, functional and symbolic rebordering. *Political Geography*, *27*(3), 301–21.

Franklin, A. (2003). The tourist syndrome. *Tourist Studies*, *3*(2), 205–17.

Freeman, A. (2005). Moral geographies and women's freedom: Rethinking freedom discourse in the Moroccan context. In Falah, G.-W., and Nagel, C. (Eds.). *Geographies of Muslim women: Gender, religion, and space*. New York: Guilford Press, 147–77.

FMV. (n.d.). *Marhaba operation*. Mohamed V Foundation for Solidarity. Retrieved 22 February 2022, from https://www.fm5.ma/en/operations/marhaba-operation.

Galani-Moutafi, V. (2000). The self and the other: Traveler, ethnographer, tourist. *Annals of Tourism Research*, *27*(1), 203–24.

Garvey, P. (2001). Driving, drinking and daring in Norway. In Miller, D. (Ed.). *Car cultures*. London: Berg, 133–52.

Girard, M. (2006). Invention de la tradition et authenticité sous le Protectorat au Maroc. L'action du Service des Arts indigènes et de son directeur Prosper Ricard. *Socio-anthropologie*, *19*. https://doi.org/10.4000/socio-anthropologie.563.

Guénif Souilamas, N. 2000. *Des 'Beurettes' Aux Descendantes d'immigrants Nord-Africains*. Paris: Bernard Grasset.

Henry, L., and Mohan, G. (2003). Making homes: The Ghanaian diaspora, institutions and development. *Journal of International Development*, *15*(5), 611–22.

Kelner, S. (2010). *Tours that bind: Diaspora, pilgrimage, and Israeli birthright tourism*. New York: New York University Press.

Khan, V.S. (1977). The Pakistanis: Mirpuri villagers at home and in Bradford. In Watson, J.L. (Ed.). *Between two cultures: Migrants and minorities in Britain*. Oxford: Blackwell, 57–89.

King, R., Christou, A., and Levitt, P. (Eds.). (2014). *Links to the diasporic homeland: Second generation and ancestral 'return' mobilities*. London: Routledge.

Ksikes, D., Peraldi, M., Rahmi, A., & El Mezouaghi, A. (2009). Classe moyenne. La grande inconnue. *TelQuel: Le Maroc Tel Qu'il Est*, *364*.

Lacoste-Dujardin, C. (1992). *Yasmina et Les Autres de Nanterre et d'ailleurs : Filles de Parents Maghrébins En France*. Paris: La Découverte.

Landau, R. (1952). *Portrait of Tangier*. London: Robert Hale.

Lepoutre, D. (1997). *Coeur de Banlieue : Codes, Rites et Langages*. Paris: O. Jacob.

Lesthaeghe, R. (Ed.). (2000). *Communities and generations: Turkish and Moroccan populations in Belgium*. Brussels: NIDI/CBGS Publications.

Levitt, P. (2002). The ties that change: Relations to the ancestral home over the life cycle. In Levitt, P., and Waters, M.C. (Eds.). *The changing face of home: The transnational lives of the second generation*. New York: Russell Sage Foundation, 123–44.

Levitt, P., and Waters, M.C. (Eds.). (2002). *The changing face of home: The transnational lives of the second generation*. New York: Russell Sage Foundation.

Light, D. (2015). Heritage and tourism. In Waterton, E., and Watson, S. (Eds.). *The Palgrave handbook of contemporary heritage research*. London: Palgrave Macmillan, 144–58.

MacCannell, D. (1973). Staged authenticity: Arrangements of social space in tourist settings. *American Journal of Sociology*, *79*(3), 589–603.

Manço, A. (1999). *Intégration et Identités : Stratégies et Positions Des Jeunes Issus de l'immigration*. Paris, Bruxelles: DeBoeck Université.

Massey, D. (2005). *For space*. London: Sage.

Marschall, S. (Ed.). (2017). *Tourism and memories of home: Migrants, displaced people, exiles and diasporic communities*. Clevedon: Channel View.

McCabe, S. (2005). Who Is a Tourist?, *Tourist Studies* 5(1): 85–106.

Merriman, P. (2009). Automobility and the geographies of the car. *Geography Compass*, *3*(2), 586–99.

Miller, D. (2001). Driven societies. In Miller, D. (Ed.). *Car cultures*. London: Berg, 1–34.

Minca, C., and Wagner, L.B. (2016). *Moroccan dreams: Orientalist myth, colonial legacy*. London: I.B. Tauris.

Modood, Tariq, Anna Triandafyllidou, and Ricard Zapata-Barrero, eds. 2006. *Multiculturalism, Muslims and Citizenship: A European Approach*. London: Routledge.

Mohan, G. (2006). Embedded cosmopolitanism and the politics of obligation: The Ghanaian diaspora and development. *Environment and Planning A*, *38*, 867–83.

Nash, C. (2008). *Of Irish descent: Origin stories, genealogy, and the politics of belonging*. Syracuse, NY: Syracuse University Press.

Ouali, N. (ed.). (2004). *Trajectoires et Dynamiques Migratoires Des Marocains de Belgique*. Louvain-La Neuve, BE: Bruylant-Academia.

Panagakos, A. (2016). Tourist, local, or other?: Greek Canadian women and the heritage fling in Greece. *Gender, Place & Culture*, *23*(2), 288–300.

Pennell, C.R. (2000). *Morocco since 1830: A history*. London: C. Hurst & Co.

Potter, R.B., & Phillips, J. (2006). Both black and symbolically white: The 'Bajan-Brit' return migrant as post-colonial hybrid. *Ethnic and Racial Studies*, *29*(5), 901–27.

Ramirez, M., Skrbiš, Z., and Emmison, M. (2007). Transnational family reunions as lived experience: Narrating a Salvadoran autoethnography. *Identities*, *14*(4), 411–31.

Reed, A. (2014). *Pilgrimage tourism of diaspora Africans to Ghana*. New York: Routledge.

Rojek, C. (1993). *Ways of escape: Modern transformations in leisure and travel*. Basingstoke: Macmillan.

Saldanha, A. (2007). *Psychedelic white*. Minneapolis: University of Minnesota Press.

Schaeffer, F. (2001). Mythe du retour et réalité de l'entre-deux la retraite en France, ou au Maroc. *Revue Européenne Des Migrations Internationales*, *17*(1), 165–76.

Sheller, M. (2004). Mobile publics: Beyond the network perspective. *Environment and Planning D: Society and Space*, *22*(1), 39–52.

Stephenson, M.L. (2002). Travelling to the ancestral homelands: The aspirations and experiences of a UK Caribbean community. *Current Issues in Tourism*, *5*(5), 378–425.

———. (2006). Travel and the "freedom of movement": Racialised encounters and experiences amongst ethnic minority tourists in the EU. *Mobilities*, *1*(2), 285–306.

Stewart, K. (2007). *Ordinary affects*. Durham; London: Duke University Press.

———. (1996). *A space on the side of the road: Cultural poetics in an 'other' America*. Princeton, NJ: Princeton University Press.

Stuart, G.H. (1955). *The international city of Tangier*. Stanford Books in World Politics. Stanford, CA: Stanford University Press.

Thrift, N. (2004). Driving in the city. *Theory, Culture & Society*, *21*(4–5), 41–59.

Tribalat, M. (1995). *Faire France : Une Grande Enquête Sur Les Immigrés et Leurs Enfants*. Paris: Editions La Découverte.

Truitt, A. (2008). On the back of a motorbike: Middle-class mobility in Ho Chi Minh City, Vietnam. *American Ethnologist*, 35(1), 3–19.

Urry, J. (1990). *The tourist gaze: Leisure and travel in contemporary societies*. London: Sage.

Velayutham, S., and Wise, A. (2005). Moral economies of a translocal village: Obligation and shame among South Indian transnational migrants. *Global Networks*, 5(1), 27–47.

Wagner, L.B. (2008). Diasporic visitor, diasporic tourist: Post-migrant generation Moroccans on holiday at "home" in Morocco. *Civilisations, Tourisme, Mobilités et Altérités Contemporaines*, 57(1–2), 191–205.

———. (2015). Using silence to "pass": Embodiment and interactional categorization in a diasporic context. *Multilingua – Journal of Cross-Cultural and Interlanguage Communication*, 34(5), 659–86.

———. (2017a). Flirting diasporically: Visits "home" facilitating diasporic encounters and complex communities. *Journal of Ethnic and Migration Studies*, 44(2), 321–40.

———. (2017b). Travelling beauty: Diasporic development and transient service encounters at the salon. In Rickly, J., Hnnam, K., and Mostafanezhad, M. (Eds.). *Tourism and leisure mobilities: Politics, work, and play*. Abingdon: Routledge, 167–77.

———. (2018). Choosing teams: Imagining futures of diaspora through the 2018 World Cup. *African Diaspora*, 11(1–2), 179–92.

———. (2019). Contingently elite: Affective practices of diasporic urban nightlife consumption. *Urban Geography*, 40(5), 665–83.

Wagner, L.B., and Minca, C. (2014). Rabat retrospective: Colonial heritage in a Moroccan urban laboratory. *Urban Studies*, 51(14), 3011–25.

Wise, A., and Velayutham, S. (2008). Second-generation Tamils and cross-cultural marriage: Managing the translocal village in a moment of cultural rupture. *Journal of Ethnic and Migration Studies*, 34(1), 113–31.

Wolbert, B. (2001). The visual production of locality: Turkish family pictures, migration and the creation of virtual neighbourhood. *Visual Anthropology Review*, 17(1), 21–35.

World Bank. (n.d.). Passenger Cars (per 1000 People) – World Development Indicators. Retrieved 26 October 2010 from http://data.worldbank.org/indicator/IS.VEH.PCAR.P3.

Wright, G. (1991). *The politics of design in French colonial urbanism*. Chicago, IL: University of Chicago Press.

4 Conclusions

Assembling diasporic mobilities

i Becoming more than the sum of parts

> **Fieldnote extract 4.1 At the Ceuta border post, 20 August 2008**
>
> arriving at the border, unbelievably, I find [Family C] who are regroup-
> ing before joining the queue. I recognize Sabah first, of course, in bright
> pink marrakshia and black round-tied headscarf. they were waiting for
> her sister's car, which is now there, so almost ready to depart. I only
> have time to say hello to everyone (Amina is really surprised to see me,
> I'm equally surprised to see them.)
>
> they left late (11 am instead of 8) had lunch at a spot on the way and
> are now here at 7/7:15 pm. mom has been crying, and I wonder if it is
> because she's leaving her family, but Amina says it's because her father
> was driving too hard (fast) and it upsets her. they are off shortly after.

This story has been an ethnography of summer holiday, compositing the
experiences of many individuals and families to show the ways this collective
practice happens year after year. As a periodic story, repeating annually, its
closing draws around again to the next opening. Rounding off the excitement
of departing toward Morocco is the disappointment and resignation of
returning home. Running into Family C at this anticlimactic moment
(Fieldnote Extract 4.1), part way through their long drive back to the
Netherlands, was my only view into the closing of this story – since I didn't
have a chance to drive back 'home' with any of the participants I followed –
and serves as the closing of my version of it. Specifically, it helps to show,
first, how *viscosity* and *insha'allah* act as affects and practices that keep this
holiday going right to its end and, second, how a malleable conceptualization
of 'diasporicness' in assemblage goes beyond the rupture of migration to
incorporate tourism and leisure mobilities.

DOI: 10.4324/9781003172383-4

Affect through practice: Insha'allah and viscosity

The 'unbelievable' encounter between me and Family C in Fieldnote Extract 4.1 helps to summarize and illustrate how *viscosity* and *insha'allah* are vital to what keeps this holiday going. The story of this book shows how many ways DVs want to have a 'real' vacation in Morocco while being protected and insulated from a Moroccan 'mentality.' That vacation happens through individuals aspiring to and enacting *insha'allah* autonomy and spontaneity, which becomes collectivized into nodes of times and spaces that are spontaneously, yet predictably, occupied by DVs on holiday. The repetition of these dynamics from family to family, individual to individual, creates patterns that feed into viscosity. DV bodies congregate around certain places at certain times and display visible marks of distinctive 'diasporicness' that make them recognizable to each other and to the larger community. This sticking together so that they dominate spaces and share affects turns them into a collectivity that is more visible and powerful than the individuals that make it up.

The serendipity of encountering Amina and her family at the border is predicated on viscous spaces of diasporic visiting, of which the European-Moroccan border is a primary example. This particular crossing point, between the Moroccan town of Castellejo and the Spanish territory of Ceuta, takes effort to reach it. It lies 2 kilometers from Castellejo's center, surrounded by a no-man's-land of barricades and police officers separating territorial Morocco from territorial Spain. Furthermore, it is a secure area; when I tried to take a picture of it, an officer approached me and watched me delete the image from my camera. Externally-resident families, crossing back and forth on European passports, constitute a significant portion of the bodies moving through this space and make it a site of *viscosity*, where it is likely I might run into someone I know.

This viscous quality of a diasporic space is not hinted at in any of the diaspora, migration, or tourism literature that I depended on in developing this project. Arriving at viscosity required, I believe, following an empirical trajectory that started by engaging with a literature based on categories and moved toward one based on assemblage – including the work of Arun Saldanha discussed in Chapter 2 ("Observing Affective Practices and Leisure as 'Diasporic'"). In part, I was able to notice it because I was moving along with *what* participants did – following their practices ethnomethodologically – rather than interrogating *why* they did it, or rather why they would claim to do so in a recorded interview. This is my central critique of most migration and diaspora literature: that it so often relies on recorded interview settings, with relatively little or no observation of practices to contextualize the attitudes described in them. People may describe their motivations or remember their actions very differently than what they might be observed to do in practice, and both the tellings and the practices can be informative when recognized as parts of a more complex story. While I do not claim to have developed an absolute and complete story of what this holiday is, I can claim to have developed a story informed by the practices I observed as a mobile ethnographer, alongside the descriptions and motivations people gave me for their practices. By tracing those practices, I arrived at the Ceuta border at the same moment as Family C and was again able to observe the viscous familiarity that populates spaces of diasporic mobilities between Morocco and Europe.

Our encounter was also part of the *insha'allah* unpredictability of the holiday in Morocco. The family themselves were participating in that dynamic – leaving later than expected, waiting for a third car to join them – but I also became part of *insha'allah* by appearing unexpectedly at the moment they were ready to cross over. I learned about *insha'allah* as an affective practice that characterizes this holiday from being told about it in participants' descriptions of their holidays, but also through experiencing it myself as part of the serendipity of following along with them during their trips. Our finding each other at that place and in that moment fits into the potentially exciting things that might happen during a trip to Morocco, which is a key part of what perpetuates this diasporic mobility among younger generations. As many examples have shown in this book, the motivation to see family has its limits; more often, the motivation to visit incorporates both the rootedness of family and the promise of *insha'allah* experiences during the holiday.

Insha'allah and *viscosity* reinforce each other as affects and practices that make this annual event work the way that it does. Moreover, I contend that they are central to what perpetuates this annual ritual as a practice for many Europeans of Moroccan origin, who might otherwise 'lose the thread' and reduce or cease their visits to Morocco. They are part of what makes this holiday more than the sum of its parts – beyond being just a vacation, or just a way to connect to one's *points de repères* in Morocco. The last snippet of conversation (Conversation 4.1) with Otman and Naim illustrates the something more that happens in Morocco, which makes this more than simply a vacation:

Conversation 4.1 A story every day

Naim and Otman B, Antwerpen, 24 March 2008, 2min		
1	N	you=know, **actually** we have a boring vacation/ just doing the same/ **every** day/ **every** year.
2	LW	then why- why keep go back? then/
3	N	because we have to!=we have our family there. (1.0) an- an- and: e-o-u- we- can go to a place, we don't have e-eh: to pay eh- a hotel,
4	LW	Yeah
5	N	we don't have/ you know, all that stuff. if you wanna go o- if you wanna eat at home, we don't have- you know/ we don't have to pay it, so actually, (.5 .h) and you meet a lot of **friends**, all your **cousins** you meet there/ (.) and you have every day beautiful weather, (1.5) °so:°
6	O	it's not eh:: just about eh::m (1.8 .h) it's true we do do- do eh: the same things every day, but (.6) every day is **another** day. so:: it's quite fun actually/ if you just- with- with all the:: **cousins** and **friends**, (.9) so::=eh: there- there happens a- a- a l[ot so::

7	N	[a **lot,** yeah/ (.3) every day hap- happens **some**thing
8	O	yeah:/ [every day is eh: like an experience, eh: you **never** forget something/ it's- really fun. real fun.
((10 turns excised))		
9	LW	like what? like e-
10	N	like ok: uh/ the next day we meet each other and we talk about ok, I we- I went last night with my **other cousins** da=da=**da**: we went to **there,** we arrived at that **city**#, (.5) you know/ that what's happened you know/ then we had a **fight,** then eh- (.4) then we had some trouble with the **police,** and we had to run **away,** and they- (.3) you know/ all those (.) stories.
11	LW	yeah. yeah.
12	N	**every**body has a story **every d[ay**
13	O	[day [ahhhehehehehe
14	LW	[hahahahah
15	N	and we're not lying too/ because **every** day **something** happens [(.8) every day.

Though this vacation is, in some ways, predictable and boring, following the same patterns every year, it is also full of stories every day. Those stories are enabled by the collective presence of many DVs following the same trajectory to and from Morocco – the friends and cousins who travel along with, in their own cars but in the same trajectory, and can be reliably found sharing the same leisure sites and participating in the same experiences. It is an obligation and a chore, and a mobility practice full of potential for new experiences.

Assembling diasporicness: Metaphors and forces

In Chapter 2, "Assembling Diasporicness," I proposed the notion of 'diasporic' predicated on the ability of individuals to be multiple ("Descent and Place as Dimensions of Diaspora"). I defined *descent* and *place* as metaphorical ways of talking about the pushes and pulls of 'blood' and 'soil' that are more malleable than more commonly used categorizational devices like ethnicity, race, racialization, religious affiliation, or nation found in migration research. In publication after publication debating the use of these terms, their definitions overlap, intersect, and sometimes contradict each other. Often, depending on which group they are applied to, they break down and fail to work as terminology. In reading Manuel DeLanda's approach to society as assemblage, I interpreted these breakdowns as a problem of imagining these concepts as stable and fixed when they need to be treated as perpetually, primordially relational and malleable. By using *descent* and *place* as separate, active entities in how individuals interact with 'Moroccanness', I am trying to complicate how I think and write about the categorical systemics involved in migration. By taking diasporic to be always evolving in assemblage, the workings of *descent* and *place* become more visible through their disjointed mappings and awkward practices, where beings and belongings should match up predictably but for some reason do not. It pushes me to think about how 'diasporicness' works in a more malleable, and less categorical, matrix.

This 'diasporicness' is interactional and emergent through practice as opposed to a pre-defined parameter that forms a community. It depends on a series of events in connection to one another: a migration from a homespace to a new place (however distant), a settling in to that new homespace while remaining somehow connected with the former one, and, as Doreen Massey and Sarah Ahmed describe, finding oneself with an inability to 'return' to the time and space previously inhabited. I use *descent* and *place* to describe the feelings, affects, actions, and practices involved in this formulation of diasporicness, but as relational and interactional, not as *a priori* definitions of belonging. By focusing on these as relational and interactional rather than definitions, I can talk about moments when individuals practice diasporic Moroccanness without defining them as always, already 'Moroccan.' It recognizes that they are more than simply 'Moroccan' – that they are multiple in their belongings.

So, when I observed Europeans of Moroccan origin; a.k.a. 'second generation' Moroccans from France, Belgium, and the Netherlands; a.k.a. diasporic visitors going on holiday in Morocco, this practice informed me about how they manage to be multiple – to be simultaneously 'Moroccan' and 'French'/'Belgian'/'Dutch', among many other things. Research by many others has shown that they also encounter significant boundaries in how they fit in Europe, which result in practices that enable them to 'integrate' there, for better or worse. By looking at how they engage with territorial Morocco, through inhabiting their ostensibly 'Moroccan' bodies and participating in 'Moroccan' spaces, I have explored how their multiplicity integrates into and encounters edges and limits to belonging in Morocco.

Based on how I observed those multiplicities to work, I organized my observations as forces of attachment, embodiment, and insulation. *Attachment* applied to elements of the holiday that often related to *descent* and *place* as a nebulous and imprecise imagining of being and connecting to one's roots in Morocco. These could be expressed through more traditionally 'diasporic' acts, like visiting family members, or, in a more expansive idea of expressing diasporic links, through practices like touring elsewhere in Morocco because it is part of one's collective 'Moroccan' history. *Embodiment* highlights 'experiential consumption' and how visitors materially and physically encounter Morocco as embodied actors. It includes moments where they are tangibly transforming themselves, like tanning in the Moroccan sun or ingesting (and maybe getting sick from) Moroccan food, as well as moments where their bodies connect with other bodies, like their cars or other DVs inhabiting the same viscous sites of leisure. *Insulation* gathered moments when separate timespaces emerged as populated by DVs, to the exclusion of others. Factors like gender and 'mentality' recur in these vignettes, in how DVs find each other to hang out and flirt with in safe, viscous spaces; but also factors of mobility, in how DVs are able to move more quickly around leisure spaces with their cars and how their cars become targets for being stopped by the police.

To present all the messy data I gathered while following DVs around during and conversing with them about their holidays, I am using attachments, embodiments, and insulations to create a structure that shows how their practices while on holiday respond to different influences. I call them 'forces' because they enact some kind of directional pressure on individuals to participate in the flow of the holiday. But the direction is not always the same: they can push and pull, attract and repel, in the way that *attachment* indexes 'family' both as rootedness and as unwanted obligations. In relation to the individuals I observed during their holidays, these forces may be part of what brings them to Morocco, but they could equally be part of what repels other Europeans of Moroccan origin from visiting Morocco at all.

Like the affective practices of *insha'allah* and *viscosity*, these forces are also acting in assemblage, reinforcing and counterbalancing each other. As they travel from European homes to Morocco becoming embodied along with their cars, those cars also insulate DVs as they move around Morocco. While touring around Morocco can be a way to express one's sense of attachment to the whole territory as a homeland, it is also an embodied experience of tasting, seeing, and being present in new sites. And, though flirting in insulated consumption spaces is a way to connect with others from similar trajectories, it is also a way that DVs can perpetuate new attachments to Morocco, as a place where new generations of family can come into being.

These forces can also contradict and interfere with each other. In particular, this appears in how insulated and embodied leisure consumption – like going on spontaneous trips, flirting in aquatic parks, and hanging out in hypermobility hopping from café to café – creates distance from family members and others resident in Morocco. These practices get associated with the 'arrogance' of having access to capital like a European visitor. In short, their consumption habits as visitors are also part of what feeds into their diasporicness – where that diasporicness is not only about being rooted there but simultaneously about being 'from outside.'

Frequenting cafés and nightclubs, exclusive beaches and hotel pools, and driving around Morocco in their own cars can be read as simply touristic consumption, reproducing economic distinctions that separate tourists from locals. These practices help me to recognize, and argue, that diasporic mobility is not necessarily motivated by being traditionally 'diasporic': it incorporates migratory imaginaries alongside other factors, like touristic leisure. Rather than frame it as 'visiting friends and relatives' or a diasporic 'return', as have many researchers who have studied similar trips by different groups, my analysis focuses as much on the crucial role that leisure consumption plays in defining this experience, even though it may start from a 'diasporic' impulse.

The internal contradictoriness of this mobility is what makes it ripe for investigation. For example, crossing over into Morocco, while it is an act motivated in part through *attachment*, can effectively create *insulation*. Embarking toward Morocco initiates a timespace in which diasporic travelers see and recognize each other engaged in the collective activity of becoming-Moroccan through visiting. While they gain momentum, crossing France and Spain as they approach the border, moving closer and closer to their end goal, their collective action acts to bind them together, separating them from their surroundings, and producing spaces for them to occupy as an embodied presence. By going to Morocco, they are also changing what 'Morocco' is. This transformation is necessary to assemblage, in that all entities and parts are shifting in relation to one another, creating a new multiplicity out of its histories, trajectories, influences, and transformations – becoming more than the sum of its parts.

ii Home for summer vacation

Any migration – to another city, another country, another continent – represents a rupture of some magnitude, shaping the distance between steps in an ordinal sequence. Something is left behind while something else is gained. In this case, an idealized 'Moroccanness' is left behind, in the unlived virtual path of children who did not grow up in Morocco (like their cousins), while other aspects are gained: European passports, consumption habits, education systems, social welfare expectations, and taste circulations. While in Morocco, diasporic visitors encounter a choice when they are interacting with others: to try to be 'Moroccan' (and sometimes fail) or to stick with what is familiar, with other diasporic Moroccan-Europeans coming from similar trajectories.

Because this visit takes place as a 'holiday' – a timespace in which visitors are seeking fun, plain and simple – the easier choice often becomes hanging out with like-minded, equally consumption-oriented familiar people. This is not to suggest that diasporic visitors do not see their families, or that family is not an important part of this holiday. Rather, as my data have shown, family is only part of it, and other aspects of the visit take up much more. In the same way that bodies can be multiple, 'home' can be appreciated in multiple ways, through both familial visits and leisure consumption.

In the end, embarking on this holiday is a practice, motivated by practical decision-making that calculates resources, like time, money, enjoyment, family, leisure, friends, hassles, mentalities, beaches, and sun, in order to choose what holiday to take this year. In essence, going 'home' to Morocco is a diasporic practice of viscosity, that takes into account the place as home and the collectivity inhabiting it temporarily, contributing to the formation of that timespace every summer.

Appendix
Methodological design*

i Interdisciplinary methods for investigating diasporic mobilities

In Chapter 2, I made some arguments about how this book intervenes in theories about diaspora and migration research by incorporating an assemblage approach. In parallel, I want to situate the methodological contribution of this book in embracing mobile methodologies (Cresswell 2012) at a disciplinary intersection between anthropology, sociolinguistics, and human geography. This intersection is predicated on my personal journey in academic training from linguistic anthropologist (Wagner 2004), to sociolinguist (Wagner 2006), and finally as a geographer (Wagner 2011), and is fundamental for how I was able to collect data and generate analyses about the diasporic summer vacation. In this section, I outline how my interdisciplinary approach frames the conclusions I am able to draw from this research.

Working in this succession of related but separable disciplines, I learned anthropological ethnographic methods for observing and analyzing social life (Agar 1996; Clifford and Marcus 1986) that prioritize developing deep and embedded understandings as a positioned researcher who spends extended time in the field. Along with that, I learned sociolinguistic and ethnomethodological approaches to differentiating how people talk about their (communicative) practices from what observably happens when they talk with each other (Blommaert 2013; Francis and Hester 2004; Garfinkel 1984). These orientations collided and merged with how *mobilities* has emerged as a field in geographical research (Cresswell 2011), drawing attention to how practices of movement and flows of people, objects, and ideas are as fundamental to social life as formations of place. But it also affected how I think about ethnography, moving from a traditional anthropological approach of long-term embedding, toward how geographers have used it alongside other qualitative methods (Davies and Dwyer 2007, 2008; Hitchings and Latham 2020) for shorter periods and investigating phenomena that are not localizable in a single place.

* A version of Section ii in this appendix was published previously in *Becoming Diasporically Moroccan* (Multilingual Matters, 2017).

While each discipline has its unique orientation, there are significant ways that they overlap. For example, strategies used in mobilities research out of geography trace back to multi-sited ethnography (Marcus 1995), an approach long advocated in anthropological research on migration or transnational communities. It provides a methodological means to embed an ethnographer in communities that are not 'located' in a single place, but in a social field which encompasses many places simultaneously (Levitt and Waters 2002; Mazzucato and Wagner 2018). This project, in fact, was originally designed in that vein as a multi-sited, 'follow-the-people' ethnography. Likewise, following sociolinguistic precedents (Blommaert 2013), I originally conceived this research as a way to investigate the complexity of diasporic individuals negotiating belonging in a 'homeland' through observing a particular activity in detail – their communicative interactions during summer vacation (Wagner 2017). What I could produce from that narrow observational scope is not an account of a whole society or community, only a slice of it through close attention to how a particular practice works for those who participate in it.

In short, though I started as an anthropologist and sociolinguist, my methods and analytical perspectives have passed through a geographical lens. Following these people and closely observing their ordinary daily communicative interactions drew me along into their ordinary, daily mobilities too. It enabled me, alongside other geographers (e.g., Bissell 2010), to consider how practices of mobility which seem to be 'in-between' departure and arrival are also lived-in social places. By paying similarly close attention to how these mobilities worked, I have been able to analyze how certain possibilities and constraints of mobility are fundamental to making and perpetuating this holiday. What emerges is an ethnography of a mobility practice – the practice of diasporic summer vacation – documenting what conditions produce and perpetuate this social world among these participants.

While some of the analyses here incorporate long-term contact and repeated encounters with participants – even intimate knowledge as a friend – many of them are based on what could be considered superficial contact in a traditional ethnographic sense. For investigating the summer vacation, the traditional idea of spending time in a single place simply would not work: the site I wanted to investigate only exists in certain times of year and is shared by many across geographical space. My analytical focus on the *practice of diasporic summer vacation* rather than on 'the diasporic community' reflects an ethnomethodological variation in ethnographic technique. Rather than producing ethnographic depth by spending extended time embedded in a community, I draw analytical conclusions through my repeated observation of practices of this 'diasporic holiday' among diverse participants and their diverse forms of participation. My objective is not to investigate the significance of the holiday for a group of individuals, but to map out how it works as a collective practice: what makes it feasible, how it comes to happen, what participants themselves see as integral to it or extraneous, and what happens if things go wrong. I am careful not to infer intentions or meanings in participants' actions or statements as analysis. The conclusions I draw here are not about why the summer holiday is important or what sort of significance it holds to the individuals implicated in it; they are about how modes of participating in this practice contribute to it, generating certain kinds of interactions, divisions, atmospheres and possibilities for encounter. This perspective is ethnomethodological insofar as I privilege participants' own understandings of this social order, from this moment in time, and this place in the world is produced through their practices.

Yet, my ability to conduct this research required ethnographic embedding and my being able to participate effectively in European-Moroccan contexts (Latham and Wagner 2021). I cultivated relationships with participants across geographical space, in Europe and in Morocco, which might last one afternoon or several years. I initially connected with diasporic communities on my first visit to Morocco in 1999 and through my subsequent education in France (2004–2006). Interspersed with this experience, I also spent time in Morocco on fieldwork for my first master's degree (2003) and on regular visits while living and studying in Europe (2004–2010). Through these personal and research experiences, I attend to the social, economic, and cultural positions of diasporic Moroccans, both inside and outside of Morocco, with which I was more able to recognize and empathize with aspects of their lives that related to diasporic belongings. My positioning is reflected in the data I gathered of my own experiences, reproduced in this book in the fieldnote extracts and photographs, alongside *in situ* ethnographic interviews in which participants describe their practices and their attitudes about them, reproduced as conversations.

In sum, the analysis I generate is shaped by my interdisciplinary and ethnographic positioning. My methodological objectives are to recognize how an act of mobility – the summer vacation – is not a sidenote to 'normal' life but part of a social order of 'diasporicness' in Morocco, and to do so by learning from participants in it how it works for them. These methodological objectives lead in part to the structure of the book as primarily a chronological account, describing the story of how this holiday takes place rather than breaking it out of its narrative arc to serve my analytical categories. That said, my analytical perspective is still present, through choosing which elements of the narrative to retell and through identifying 'forces' of attachment, embodiment, and insulation as connecting across different events of this composited holiday. This latter perspective is what I aim to contribute to conversations about the lives of diasporically-oriented individuals as conclusions I made, from my positioned observing and using my limited ethnographic depth. For that, I owe a debt of gratitude to those who participated directly in this research.

ii Participant characteristics

The primary population in this research are post-migrant generation diasporic Moroccans who reside in France, Belgium, or the Netherlands, and who participate in the annual holiday in Morocco. As such, I considered their general characteristics to include the following:

1   they identify Morocco as a 'homeland' as children of two parents who emigrated from there, but one in which they themselves have not lived beyond the age of entry into school (generally 4 years old), if at all;
2   they have some linguistic competence in a Moroccan language, but have broader competence in French, Dutch, or Flemish; and
3   they, as adults over age 18, choose to spend holiday time in Morocco, regularly or sporadically, in their hometowns or elsewhere.

Their other social characteristics vary, including gender, educational attainment, religious practice, marital status, and professional attainment. They come from different towns in Europe and travel to different hometowns in Morocco. Their central unifying characteristic is participation in the holiday, whether actively or passively.

I found participants through networks, snowball sampling, and recruitment of flow populations (Ritchie and Lewis 2003, 94). The initial source for networked and snowball participants was close relationships with three key women, one each from France, Belgium, and the Netherlands, called Families A, B, and C, respectively. I recruited other participants during fieldwork in Europe and in Morocco by approaching individuals with a survey questionnaire on language use and soliciting them for further participation. Through these combined methods, 76 individuals contributed their time and opinions for interviews, participant observation, and recordings, along with approximately 70 others who filled in survey questionnaires.[1]

During fieldwork, I stayed in the family home of each of the three key women – in France and the Netherlands for short visits and in Belgium over a six-week period in Antwerp. All of their family members were made aware of my research aims, and many of them participated in the project through interviews in Europe or through time spent with them on holiday in Morocco.

Figure A.1 identifies the form of participation of the three women and their friends and families in how they participated in the principal qualitative methods used in this project – interview, participant observation, and recording – as well as where their participation took place – in Europe, Morocco, or both. It also shows clusters of individuals I met during their summer travels, beyond the networks of these three women, who made up the remainder of the 76 I count as participants. Finally, it gives an indication of some of the non-participants who were present during the research, like migrant-generation parents, young children, and spouses or friends who are not of Moroccan origin.

The intensive participation of the three key women is reflective of their statuses and positions within their familial social groups, and my own position as a highly educated, female, American researcher. Yasmine A[2] (France) and Malika B (Belgium) are older than 30 and never married, which is relatively unusual for Moroccan women, as pressure to marry is strong in Morocco and in diaspora (Buitelaar 2007). Mouna C (Netherlands) was still relatively young (21 at the time of the research), but enrolled in advanced higher education. The two older women were in professional jobs, are both multilingual beyond their home languages in their professional capacities,

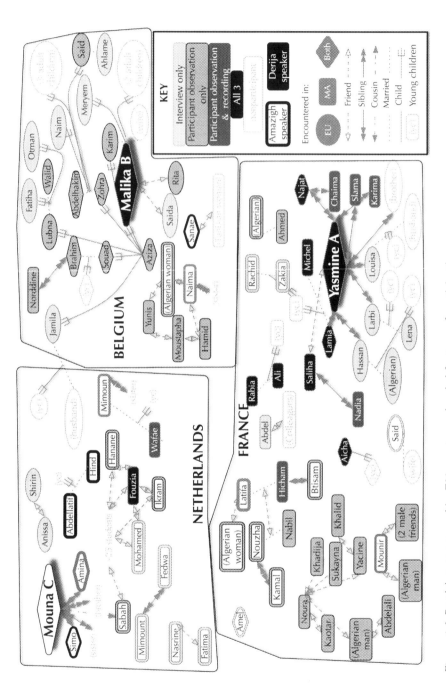

Figure A.1 Participants grouped by EU country and coded for type of participation.

and have many friends and connections outside of their immediate communities, along with regular contact with their families.

My positioning as a researcher relates very intensely to the status of these women as unusually highly educated or extroverted toward a community which we shared. Their individual interests reflect my own personal interests, to some extent, in that we all enjoy learning languages and interacting with others outside of our home communities. Yet, my status as doubly outsider – in that I am neither Moroccan, French, Belgian, nor Dutch – also served a purpose in positioning me to others beyond these women. While my interest in Moroccans was sometimes questioned or thought suspicious – either because I might be an agent of the CIA or because I could be in search of a husband – I made efforts to reassure potential participants that this was not the case.

The unusual status of these three women may make them typical examples of the ethnographic problem of access to a community only being negotiated through an atypical, fringe gatekeeper. Indeed, they were often on very different life trajectories than the siblings, cousins, and peers that I met. But through contact with their families, and sometimes extended families or family friends, I was able to recognize a cross-section of potential participants. Given my own relevant recognizable attributes, as a European-origin American, non-Muslim researcher, entry into this community would be limited no matter who might be the gatekeeper. Distrust for non-Muslims and for researchers is understandable among a minority community that has been subjected to successive microscopes and is routinely characterized as problematic in media and public administration. Like any ethnographer, what I was able to access and am able to analyze will always be limited by my backgrounds and history, the participants and their lifecourses and orientations, and those who I was not able to connect with whose experiences may show a very different story.

Participants beyond the networks of these three women were recruited by approaching individuals in Morocco during holiday periods. This was normally accomplished by spending time in high-traffic pedestrian areas or in certain cafés or restaurants that DVs tended to frequent, introducing myself as a researcher and soliciting responses to the questionnaire, then pursuing further contact with individuals who indicated willingness to participate (the last question on the survey). Interactions with these flow population participants ranged from spending an afternoon shopping in the souk, to meeting them over a period of days for various holiday activities. Yet, as Figure A.1 demonstrates, the variety of forms of participation is fairly balanced, with proportional numbers of individuals who gave their time for interviews, participant observation, and recording from each country.

iii Ethical considerations

When this project was initiated in 2004, ethical review by an external committee was not as universally assumed as part of social science research procedure as it is now. Coming from a US university at the time, where Institutional Review Boards have overseen social science as well as other kinds of 'human subjects' research, I was familiar with some practices of and expectations for ethical design as applied to anthropology. The French and British university systems who governed my research work during the periods covered in this book (2006 onwards) did not, at the time, exert comprehensive institutional requirements for ethical review. So, while I considered ethical issues in preparation for and execution of the different stages in this research, my plans and practices were not reviewed by a board. They were assessed, along with the whole of the research, by my supervisors, the committee members in my upgrade to doctoral candidate, and eventually the PhD examiners. With this in mind, I want to clarify some of the ethical practices that were in place for the stages of this project and indicate some practices that have been more widely adopted in the 20 years since I began which would have been useful for it.

Some basic principles were applied from the beginning, especially related to participation and consent. For example, I did not solicit participation from individuals under the age of 18, as their minor-aged status can bring into question their ability to consent to research investigation. Since then, I have learned more about research with youth and principles of continuous consent (Akom Ankobrey 2022; van Geel 2019), which advocate that including young people from age 15 in research is important for enabling their active voices in discourses that concern them. That said, restricting my participants to age 18 or older was not a significant methodological issue in this project, in that youth itself was not a category under investigation. I considered all participants as 'adults,' ranging in age from 18 to 50s. There were, however, children and youth under 18 who were present as family members in nearly every group. When necessary, I considered them as relevant actors in ongoing activity, but have taken care not to report their actions or behaviors with any specificity that could lead to identification. Children are present in this book inasmuch as they are present in households, but have not been the subject of investigation.

All individuals who participated actively in the research were informed about its purpose: to explore what actually happens during summer holidays in Morocco. Individuals who were recorded in interviews or wore microphones in 'naturally occurring' settings gave oral consent to being recorded. I did not require written consent forms because they had a strong potential to establish *distrust* among participants who have been subjected to stigmatization in other ways. Having informed participants about my purposes, I took their continued willingness to interact with me as consent. This was reinforced by the occasions when my requests for interaction were turned down or avoided by potential participants who I had approached, which indicated their choice not to participate.

Another factor I identified in the original plans for this research is the expectation of hospitality in Moroccan households. From my first visit to Morocco, I was welcomed to stay in private homes though I was little more than an acquaintance. While I stayed as a guest of some participants with whom I had a longer-term and more substantial relationship beyond the research, I also shared accommodation with others, both in visiting at their homes and in offering my housing space when I could. This kind of intimate shared private space opens questions about both consent, in terms of what an ethnographer might be allowed to witness as 'data,' and in the safety and security of the ethnographer herself. Had I had the terminology at the time, I would have practiced more explicit forms of 'continuous consent' (Klykken 2021), both as a household guest and as a way to involve participants more actively in the purpose of the research. That said, I tried to be sensitive to moments when my presence in the household as a guest meant I was witness to private activities that I should not record as a researcher.

As an additional layer to consent, since completing fieldwork and beginning to publish research articles based on this data, I have 'member-checked' or validated (Ritchie and Lewis 2003) some of the analyses with participants who continue to be close contacts. Member-checking serves both to ensure their consent in producing analyses that concern them and as a way to gauge how my conclusions relate to members of the target population who may be affected by their publication. Unfortunately, it has not always been possible to check with participants directly involved, as the contact information I gathered for some participants has expired over time. In these cases, I take extra care to ensure that no combination of details published about them can triangulate their precise identity, to protect their anonymity a step further than using a pseudonym. As much as the landscape of ethical research practice has changed since this research was initially executed, so has the capacity to extrapolate identifying information from even minor informational traces. While I cannot absolutely guarantee anonymity in this regard, I have manipulated some details so that, hopefully, individuals cannot be identified.

As part of "following the people" in their mobilities, the pool of participants was ephemeral and unpredictable – so, again, not in line with what is normally expected of ethnographic research that takes place in a co-located and circumscribed community. However, I contend that both the shorter and longer encounters I have had with participants contribute to developing ethnographic depth, leading to the analyses I make in this book because it is about the practice of summer vacation and not about the 'community.' The composition of a diasporic holiday is made up of different actors each successive summer, in terms of who decides to travel, and where and when they go. While I had initially imagined a 'community' of participants, whom I would interview in Europe and then follow on holiday in Morocco, in the end, very few of those interviewed in Europe made the journey in 2008. Most of those who participated in all three qualitative collection methods did so entirely in Morocco, or across pilot and primary research. I therefore consider each participant's contribution in reference to what I know of his or her personal background, but also as a fragment of the practice of this diasporic holiday, as part of how it is shaped by those who make it happen year after year.

Notes

1 The questionnaires were not further analyzed because the sampling strategy for their collection was not sufficiently structured to produce any conclusive statistics. I used them only as secondary, background information to inform further recruitment and interview topics.
2 All names are pseudonyms.

References

Agar, M. (1996). *The professional stranger*. New York: Academic Press.

Akom Ankobrey, G.A.S. (2022). "You can't limit yourself to one country": Mobility trajectories and transnational engagements of young Dutch-Ghanaians. Doctoral Thesis, Maastricht: Maastricht University. https://doi.org/10.26481/dis. 20220602gaa.

Bissell, D. (2010). "Narrating Mobile Methodologies: Active and Passive Empiricisms." In *Mobile Methodologies*, edited by Ben Fincham, Mark McGuinness, and Lesley Murray, 53–68. London: Palgrave Macmillan. doi:10.1057/9780230281172_5.

Blommaert, J. (2013). *Ethnography, superdiversity and linguistic landscapes: Chronicles of complexity*. Clevedon: Multilingual Matters.

Buitelaar, M. (2007). Staying close by moving out. The contextual meanings of personal autonomy in the life stories of women of Moroccan descent in The Netherlands. *Contemporary Islam*, *1*(1), 259–76. https://doi.org/10.1007/s11562-007-0003-1.

Clifford, J., and Marcus, G.E. (Eds.). (1986). *Writing culture: The poetics and politics of ethnography: A School of American Research advanced seminar*. Berkeley: University of California Press.

Cresswell, T. (2011). Mobilities I: Catching up. *Progress in Human Geography*, *35*(4), 550–58. https://doi.org/10.1177/0309132510383348.

———. (2012). Mobilities II: Still. *Progress in Human Geography*, *36*(5), 645–53. https://doi.org/10.1177/0309132511423349.

Davies, G, and Dwyer, C. (2007). "Qualitative Methods: Are You Enchanted or Are You Alienated?" *Progress in Human Geography*, *31*(2): 257–66. doi:10.1177/0309132507076417.

———. (2008). "Qualitative Methods II: Minding the Gap." *Progress in Human Geography*, *32*(3): 399–406. doi:10.1177/0309132507084403.

Francis, D.J., and Hester, S. (2004). *An invitation to ethnomethodology: Language, society and interaction*. London; Thousand Oaks, CA: Sage.

Garfinkel, H. (1984). *Studies in ethnomethodology* (2nd ed.). Cambridge: Polity Press.

Hitchings, R, and Latham, A. (2020). "Qualitative Methods II: On the Presentation of 'Geographical Ethnography.'" *Progress in Human Geography*, *44*(5): 972–80. doi:10.1177/0309132519879986.

Klykken, F.H. (2021). Implementing continuous consent in qualitative research. *Qualitative Research*, May, Online. https://doi.org/10.1177/14687941211014366.

Latham, A. and Wagner, L.B. (2021). "Experiments in Becoming: Corporeality, Attunement and Doing Research." *Cultural Geographies*, *28*(1): 91–108. https://doi.org/10.1177/1474474020949550.

Levitt, O., and Waters, M.C. (Eds.). (2002). *The changing face of home: The transnational lives of the second generation*. New York: Russell Sage Foundation.

Marcus, G.E. (1995). Ethnography in/of the world system: The emergence of multi-sited ethnography. *Annual Review of Anthropology*, *24*, 95–117.

Mazzucato, V., and Wagner, L.B. (2018). "Multi-Sited Fieldwork in a Connected World." In *Handbook on the Geographies of Globalisations*, edited by Robert Kloosterman, Virginie Mamadouh, and Pieter Terhorst, 412–21. Cheltenham: Edward Elgar.

Ritchie, J., and Lewis, J. (2003). *Qualitative research practice: A guide for social science students and researchers*. London; Thousand Oaks, CA: Sage Publications.

van Geel, J.H.M. (2019). Being mobile, becoming educated: Young Ghanaians' mobility trajectories and educational experiences between Ghana and the Netherlands. Doctoral Thesis, Maastricht: Maastricht University. https://doi.org/10.26481/dis.20190509jg.

Wagner, L.B. (2004). Tourism and representation in Morocco: The mediation of authenticity through language, interaction, and video. Master's thesis, Austin, TX: University of Texas at Austin.

———. (2006). Les pratiques langagières de jeunes d'origine Marocaine au Maroc. Enquête sure les compétences linguistiques aux marches. Mémoire de Masters 2 Recherche, Paris: Université René Descartes – Paris V.

———. (2011). Negotiating diasporic mobilities and becomings: Interactions and practices of Europeans of Moroccan descent on holiday in Morocco. Doctoral thesis, London: University College London.

———. (2017). *Becoming diasporically Moroccan: Linguistic and embodied practices for negotiating belonging*. Clevedon: Multilingual Matters.

Index

Pages in *italics* refer to figures and pages followed by "n" refer to notes.

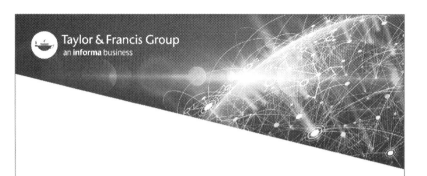